Leadership and Change in the 21st Century

Leadership and Change in the 21st Century

A Synthesis of Modern Theory, Research, and Practice

Robert E. Levasseur, Ph.D.

MindFire Press
Annapolis, Maryland

ISBN–13: 978–0–9789930–0–9
ISBN–10: 0–9789930–0–4

Library of Congress Control Number: 2006908871

Published by MindFire Press of Annapolis, Maryland
(www.mindfirepress.com)

"The mind is a fire to be kindled,
not a vessel to be filled."

Plutarch

Table of Contents

Preface

This is really two books in one. The first—*The Science of Modern Leadership*—uses theory and research to make the case for a new form of leadership. One with the potential to enable us to work together to meet the challenges of the 21st century. The second—*The 21st Century Leader in Action*—provides insights into how a leader might apply this modern form of leadership to effect positive social change in an increasingly interconnected, interdependent world.

The reason for incorporating two books in one is to avoid a shortcoming of most books on the subject. Most leadership books fall into two broad categories. Either they dwell on theory at the expense of practice, or practice at the expense of theory. The former tend to be general and descriptive because the authors have not put their ideas to the test of practical application. The latter, while they are detailed and prescriptive, are often biased and simplistic because their authors base them largely on personal experience or pet theories, rather than grounding them broadly in the literature of leadership, management, and change.

Because of its unique structure, there are two ways to read this book. You can either start by reading part I (theory) or part II (practice), depending on your interest and needs. Later you can read the other part to further your understanding of the subject. Social scientist researchers and others interested in the theoretical underpinnings of modern leadership will probably read the book as written, since the progression from theory and research to practice will feel more natural to them. Conversely, managers and others more interested in how to lead may be inclined to start with part II. The choice is yours.

Part I

The Science of Modern Leadership

Chapter 1

The Tectonic Plates Are Shifting

What is wrong with our leaders today? The world is changing dramatically, yet many persist in applying traditional leadership methods that no longer seem to work. In effect, they continue to look under the street-light for keys lost in a dark alley. Why? Perhaps it is easier and less risky, enabling them to claim they are taking action, however futile it may be.

Are they causing society harm in the process? Some leadership experts, like Warren Bennis, think they are:

> Thanks to globalization we can now talk about the end of leadership as we know it without the risk of hyperbole . . . top-down leadership is not only wrong, unrealistic, and maladaptive, but also dangerous. This obsolete form of leadership will erode competitive advantage and destroy the aspirations of any leader or organization . . . . This top-down tendency is dysfunctional in today's world of blurring change and will get us into unspeakable trouble unless we understand that the search engine for effective change is the workforce and their creative alliance with top leadership. (Bennis, 1999, pp. 7–8)

Bennis is not alone. Over 25 years ago, James McGregor Burns, a Pulitzer Prize-winning political scientist, argued that there was a "crisis in leadership" due to "the mediocrity or irresponsibility of so many men and women in power" (Burns, 1978, p. 1) and responded to the threat this posed to society by calling for a new, transformative style of leadership that would engage followers in the change process by appealing to their higher level needs.

> I describe leadership here as no mere game among elitists and no mere populist response but as a structure of action that engages persons, to varying degrees, throughout the levels and among the interstices of society. Only the inert, the alienated, and the powerless are unengaged . . . . Leadership is nothing if not linked to collective purpose (and) the effectiveness of leaders must be judged not by their press clippings but by actual social change measured by intent and by the satisfaction of human needs and expectations. (Burns, 1978, p. 3)

Since Burns coined the term "transforming leadership" and, in effect, issued a challenge to leaders and leadership pundits everywhere, many people have called for new, more engaging forms of leadership to augment or replace traditional, top-down leadership models (Abrashoff, 2001; Ackoff, 1999; Bass, 1990; Bennis, 1999; Burns, 1978; Cleveland, 2000; Gronn, 1997; Handy, 1980; Louis, 1994; Neal & Conhaim, 2000; Somerset, 2000; Weidman, 2002). However, despite the urging of these and many other leadership scholars and practitioners, traditional forms of leadership persist in many organizations today. Sadly, the recent Enron scandal speaks both to the persistence of top-down leadership and its potentially "dangerous" effects.

While many leaders cling tenaciously to what they know, the tectonic plates of social change continue to shift dramatically. The signs are everywhere, from the far-reaching impact of the PC and the Internet to the undeniable effects of instantaneous communication and rapid transportation to and from all corners of the globe.

The result of these revolutionary changes is a massive and inevitable social movement from the old world of isolated, dependent followers to the new world of interconnected, interdependent participants in a global community. If history repeats itself, which may well occur unless leaders recognize and respond appropriately to this new social condition, the pressure for meaningful, collaborative change toward a "collective purpose" will build inexorably and eventually erupt in unpredictable and perhaps undesirable ways.

How can we effectively cope with this historical societal transformation? A clear first step is to acknowledge the need for a dramatic response. However, this begs the question of what to do and how to make whatever we decide to do happen?

Unfortunately, leadership pundits have no real answers to this question, since the problem is new and the paradigms in vogue are old. What we need is a new leadership paradigm, one commensurate in power and sophistication to the nature of this global imperative. Fortunately for us, as we shall see, our great thinkers have provided us with the elements of such a paradigm.

Chapter 2

The New Leadership Paradigm

Thomas Kuhn (1962/2004) used the term paradigm to describe a tradition of scientific inquiry, such as Copernican astronomy or Newtonian dynamics, based on an unprecedented new view of the world which better explains the mysteries that scientists seek to resolve while leaving many unresolved problems for its practitioners to study (p. 10). In this context, a scientific revolution is the result of a dramatic movement to adopt a new paradigm—a paradigm shift.

To meet the challenges of the 21st century, we need to replace the increasingly dysfunctional, command-and-control, top-down style prevalent today with a new leadership paradigm. Fortunately for us, the essential elements of this new paradigm are becoming more and more evident. Furthermore, the advocates of each, as we shall see, include many eminent social science scholars, such as Burns, Boyer, Lewin, and Maslow.

Element One: A Systemic World View

> The concept of "system" constitutes a new "paradigm," in Thomas Kuhn's phrase, or . . . a "new philosophy of nature" contrasting the "blind laws of nature" of the mechanistic world view and the world process as a Shakespearean tale told by an idiot, with an organismic outlook of the "world as a great organization." (Bertalanffy, 1968, p. *xxi*)

Who has not heard the expression that the whole is greater than the sum of its parts? Who does not believe that an automobile or TV set is more than a collection of its component parts? Who does not believe that a human being is more than a collection of organs? Yet many of our leaders continue to act as if the world is not an interconnected whole (i.e., a complex system made up of many interrelated elements or subsystems). Why?

While no one can answer this question definitively, for our purposes it is instructive to examine three of the reasons why our leaders seem to ignore the systemic nature of the world on a regular basis. First, it is often in their interest to do so. After all, most leaders have a constituency whose interests they have promised to advocate.

Second, most problems are complicated. Therefore, to solve them, people try to simplify them. One common strategy is to divide a complicated problem into several manageable parts and work on each separately. The final solution is then, hopefully, a composite of the individual component solutions. Sometimes this works well (generally, when the components of the system are only loosely coupled), but sometimes it doesn't (especially when they are highly interconnected).

Third, many people depend almost exclusively on logic when making decisions, basing their decisions solely on an analysis of the tangible, measurable aspects of a problem or situation. While there is nothing inherently wrong with this approach, it can, if not balanced with an intuitive sense of the importance of other intangible factors (such as people's needs and concerns), lead to bad decisions.

While there are many reasons why people, including leaders of organizations and countries, fail to think systemically, doing so, according to eminent system thinker, Ervin Laszlo, is imperative for those who want to effect positive social change. Like Ludwig von Bertalanffy (1968), Laszlo (1996) viewed system theory as a worldview with the potential to guide the collective decision making process in significant ways.

> We cannot expect to satisfy all the requirements attaching to a worldview in reference to science alone, without also drawing on the insights of religion and the values of humanism, but . . . the new systems view can provide the clues, the metaphors, the orientations, and even the detailed models for solving critical problems on this precious but increasingly crowded and exploited planet. (Laszlo, 1996, p. 13)

Element Two: A Transformative Vision

Will an incremental vision of local change get the job done? Or is a truly inspirational vision of systemic transformation needed to fuel the required changes? While this may seem like a rhetorical question, ask yourself how many of our leaders attempt to engage us in what Burns (1978, p. 3) called a "collective purpose," an adventure so great and worth participating in that it moves us to action?

Compare the feeling engendered by such a compelling vision to the one engendered by yet another politician appealing to a perceived special interest or by another corporate leader extolling the virtues of the bottom line? Paraphrasing Mark Twain, the difference between a transformative vision and a partisan view is like the difference between lightning and the lightning bug.

Experts in leadership and change agree on the power of vision and the need for leaders to put forth compelling, transformative visions to engage system members (followers) in the change process (Bass, 1990; Bradford & Cohen, 1984; Senge, 1990; Weisbord & Janoff, 1995; Abshire, 2001; Carl & Javidian, 2001). For example, Bass (1990) distinguished between so-called transactional leaders (who focus on doing things right) and transformational leaders (who focus on doing the right things). The former strive to optimize the efficiency of an organization, while the latter strive to maximize the effectiveness of the organization.

According to Avolio, Waldman, and Yammarino (1991, p. 9), the four key elements of transformational leadership are (a) individualized consideration, (b) intellectual stimulation, (c) inspirational motivation, and (d) idealized influence. In practice, this means that a leader must focus on the emotional and developmental needs of each person, provide intellectual stimulation in the form of innovative ideas and approaches, and strive to "attain charisma" in the eyes of the followers (Bass, 1990, p. 21). Most importantly, transformational leaders must learn to "share the vision" if they want to "inspire, energize, and intellectually stimulate their employees" (Bass, 1990, p. 19).

Bradford and Cohen (1984) underscored the importance of shared vision or collective purpose to transforming leadership by including it in their three keys to managing for organizational excellence. Peter Senge, author of The Fifth Discipline, described the critical importance of common or shared vision as follows:

> If any one idea about leadership has inspired organizations for thousands of years, it's the capacity to hold a shared picture of the future we seek to create. One is hard pressed to think of any organization that has sustained some measure of greatness in the absence of goals, values, and missions that become deeply shared throughout the organization. (Senge, 1990, p. 9)

A visionary leader who practices inspirational motivation by creating and sharing a compelling vision of the future will appear to be charismatic to followers. Carl and Javidian (2001), who studied the universality of charismatic leadership across national boundaries, found that "a relatively culture-free charismatic leader profile does exist" and that "it is comprised of the constructs of a vision, motivation, and proactivity" (p. B1).

So the ability to create and effectively share a compelling, systemic, transformative vision of the future is an essential and universally recognized attribute of the transforming leader. But is it enough to catalyze and ensure meaningful organizational or social change? As we shall see, it is a necessary but not sufficient condition. Fortunately, the third and fourth elements of our new paradigm for transformative societal change, which deal directly with the very nature of the change process, remedy this shortcoming and complete the new paradigm.

Element Three: Integrative Scholarship

Where will we get the creative new systemic ideas needed to transform society? Will we have to wait for scientists to discover yet another technological marvel, the equivalent of a miracle cure for what ails society? Or is there another possibility? Ernest Boyer, a renowned scholar, suggests an answer in what he calls the scholarship of integration.

> By integration, we mean making connections across the disciplines, placing the specialties in a larger context, illuminating data in a revealing way . . . . Those engaged in discovery ask, "What is to be known, what is yet to be found?" Those engaged in integration ask, "What do the findings *mean*?" Is it possible to provide a larger, more comprehensive understanding? (Boyer, 1990, pp. 18–19)

What Boyer suggests goes far beyond inviting experts in many fields of knowledge to individually apply their specialized knowledge to the solution of a particular problem. Boyer's integrative scholarship calls for a systemic perspective, one that requires all participants to collectively draw upon and synthesize the theories, research, and practices of all of the disciplines necessary to solve the problem. In short, Boyer's integrative scholar or integrative leader, whether man or woman, is more like a "Renaissance Man" than a traditional leader.

Although integrating vast amounts of knowledge across numerous disciplines may seem like a daunting task, according to Boyer it is already occurring in many areas:

> Today, more than at any time in recent memory, researchers feel the need to move beyond traditional disciplinary boundaries, communicate with colleagues in other fields, and discover patterns that connect. . . . (There is) evidence that an intellectual sea change may be occurring, one that is perhaps as momentous as the nineteenth-century shift in the hierarchy of knowledge, when philosophy gave way more firmly to science. Today, interdisciplinary and integrative studies, long on the edges of academic life, are moving toward the center, responding both to new intellectual questions and to pressing human problems. (Boyer, 1990, pp. 20–21)

If they want to catalyze meaningful solutions to these pressing problems, tomorrow's leaders must follow the lead of academicians and make integrative thinking a core competency.

Element Four: A Collaborative Process

As we have seen, the leadership literature emphasizes the importance to transforming leadership of creating an engaging, shared vision. Not surprisingly, the change management literature supports this view. Elrod and Tippett (2002) compared and contrasted 15 change models from the literatures of organizational change and personal development in an attempt to determine consistencies among them and, if possible, synthesize their core concepts into a coherent macro model of change. They were able to fit the majority of these models (i.e., 13 out or 15) into a basic, three-stage pattern consisting of an initial equilibrium, a disruptive transition period, and a final equilibrium that "follow Lewin's 1952 three-phase model of change" (Elrod & Tippett, 2002).

Kurt Lewin was the principal architect of many of the theories underlying modern change management and organization development (Burke, 1982; Marrow, 1969; Schein, 1999). One of the most important of the Lewin theories is the simple and elegant three-step change model consisting of (a) unfreezing, (b) movement, and (c) refreezing (Burke, 1987, pp. 54–56) referred to by Elrod and Tippett (2002).

Not surprisingly, leadership experts differ about the best way to initiate the change process and unfreeze a situation. A minority argue for a more confrontational approach, one that entails creating a crisis to stimulate a sense of urgency in followers (Day, 1999; Heifetz & Linsky, 2002; Kotter, 1996; Kotter & Cohen, 2002). Others prefer a less conflict inducing, more participative approach; one that involves the creation of a common or shared vision of what is possible if people work together (i.e., collaborate) to achieve common goals

(Abrashoff, 2001; Ackoff, 1999; Bennis, 1999; Bradford & Cohen, 1984; Burke, 1982; Marrow, 1969; Senge, 1990; Somerset, 2001).

Support for a vision-based, collaborative approach to unfreezing a situation and engaging system members in the change process comes from the literature of group management. Johnson and Johnson (1989) did a meta-analysis of over 500 research studies of the effect of conflict versus cooperation on performance and satisfaction and found that "generally achievement and productivity were higher in cooperative situations than in competitive or individualistic ones" (p. 171).

The meta-analysis of Johnson and Johnson (1989) also supports the emphasis of transforming leadership on group goals (collective purpose) and teamwork, since a cooperative process tends to facilitate the second or movement phase of the change management process. Thus, transforming leadership, by employing vision to unfreeze a situation and cooperation to facilitate change, capitalizes on the inherent power of collaborative processes to effect change.

The evidence in support of a collaborative process as the means of effecting positive organizational and social change is clear. When coupled with the other three elements of the new transformative change paradigm, the combination is formidable. In effect, each element of the new leadership paradigm is necessary, but not sufficient to the task at hand. However, collectively the four elements of the paradigm collectively constitute a prescription for effecting positive change.

The New Paradigm in Perspective

To change his or her world (e.g., family, team, organization, or society), a leader starts with a systemic (big picture) view that takes into account the components and how they interconnect to form an organic whole. Next, he or she creates a compelling vision of the future that engages the members of the system in a collective purpose. To paraphrase Isaac Newton and Ernest Boyer, the leader then stands on the shoulders of giants by using an integrative scholarship that draws on all of the relevant theories, research, and practices available to inform the change process. Finally, he or she engages followers in a collaborative change process that puts them squarely in the picture and harnesses their ideas and energy to manifest the shared vision.

Chapter 3

Leadership & Change: An Integrative View

The new leadership paradigm provides transforming leaders everywhere with the essential elements of a new approach to effecting significant, positive organizational and social change. But how exactly do they go about doing it?

What transforming leaders really need to get this vital job done is a leadership model which incorporates the elements of the new paradigm and guides them step by step through the process of catalyzing and managing transformative change. Following the tenets of Boyer's scholarship of integration, we search for additional clues to such an integrative perspective on leadership and change in the forest of ideas that is the domain of leadership theory, research, and practice.

Judging from the historical development of the field, the precise nature of leadership is problematic. Beginning with the notion that a true leader is a "great man" with certain admirable traits (e.g., intelligence and self-confidence), progressing to leadership theories based on behaviors (such as having a democratic versus an autocratic style), and continuing through today in a dizzying array of alternative theories (e.g., situational leadership, visionary leadership, team-based leadership, charismatic leadership, transformational leadership, ethical leadership, principle-centered leadership, and servant leadership), the state of current knowledge in the leadership field brings to mind the story of the blind men and the elephant.

Donelle Blubaugh (2002) retold the ancient tale of six old, blind men in India who argued with conviction about the nature of an elephant, each claiming to know for certain what it was—a wall, a snake, a spear, a cow, a carpet, a piece of rope—based on an examination of one of its main features—its side, trunk, tusk, leg, ear, or tail, respectively. This noisy argument among many self-proclaimed elephant experts is reminiscent of the often divergent claims made by experts in the field of leadership over the years. With all of this confusion and contradiction, it has been as difficult for a coherent leadership model to emerge as it was for the Rajah to get a nap in the presence of these unruly, opinionated old men. Fortunately for us, the Rajah's sage advice is as valid today as it was long ago:

> How can you be so certain you are right? The elephant is a very large animal. Each man touched only one part. Perhaps, if you put the parts together, you will see the truth. Now, let me finish my nap in peace. (Blubaugh, 2002, pp. 1–3)

So let's follow the Rajah's advice and critically examine from an integrative perspective the ideas of a number of classical and contemporary theorists, researchers, and practitioners in an effort to find the ones which will enable us to determine how to implement the new paradigm for transformative social change.

Overview

Our search for a new leadership model will focus on three central questions:

- What is leadership?
- How do individuals, organizations, and societies change?
- What is the relationship between leadership and change?

Two simple beliefs or principles will guide the search for answers to these questions. The first is that the answers already exist in the intersection of theories, research, and practices of several related fields, and that what is needed is a creative synthesis of existing knowledge, an "integration" formed by "making connections across disciplines, placing the specialties in a larger context" thereby providing "a larger, more comprehensive understanding" (Boyer, 1990, p. 29).

The second guiding principle is that the breakthroughs in thinking which the answers to these fundamental questions about leadership and change represent are possible only through a "paradigm shift"—a fundamental change of perspective of the kind described by Kuhn (1962/2004) and reflected in the elements of the new paradigm for transformative change presented in the preceding chapter.

Thus, in this chapter we will lay the groundwork for a new, integrative, step-by-step leadership model by examining what social scientists have to say about (a) human behavior and development (i.e., individual change), and (b) leadership and change. Then, we will synthesize from these creative ideas an integrative leadership model which is consistent with prior theory, research, and practice, and which incorporates the four elements of the new paradigm for transformative change.

Social Scientists re Human Development

Leaders lead people. People effect change. Hence, at its core, leadership and change are about people. The place to begin our exploration of the nature of leadership and change is, therefore, by examining relevant theories and research about human behavior and development (i.e., individual change). We start with the groundbreaking work of Kurt Lewin.

Lewin's Behavior Model

One of the most profound early thinkers in the field of human development, Kurt Lewin, espoused a simple and elegant view of human behavior that serves admirably as a lens for viewing all subsequent work in the field.

> Lewin maintained that applications of field theory were possible in all branches of psychology. He viewed the life space as the psychologist's universe. In it, person and environment are interrelated and individual behavior is always derived from the relation of the concrete individual to the concrete situation. Behavior, therefore, is a function of the life

> space: B = f (LS), which in turn is a product of the interaction between the person, P, and his (or her) environment, E. (Marrow, 1969, p. 38)

Thus, Lewin's model of human behavior relates personality and environment as follows:

$$B = f(P \cdot E). \tag{1}$$

Lewin's model suggests that, in the same environment, two people with different personalities may respond differently to the same stimuli. Conversely, the same person may behave quite differently in different environments.

Several simple examples may help to clarify the meaning of Lewin's model. First, consider the behavior of an innately friendly person at a party versus that of an innately unfriendly person. All other things being equal, the friendly person is likely to be quite open and warm towards the other guests. The unfriendly person, on the other hand, in an identical environment, is likely to be much less engaging. We, therefore, observe different behavior in the same environment due to fundamental differences in the personalities of the two individuals.

Second, consider the behavior of the friendly person during an attempted mugging after the party. In this new environment, despite his or her innate sense of openness to others, the otherwise friendly person is likely to be quite hostile toward the muggers. Hence, we observe different behavior in different environments from the same person.

Lewin's model tells us that human behavior is a result of the interaction of the individual and environment. As we shall see, other great thinkers in the field of human development, including Bronfenbrenner and Maslow, agreed with Lewin. We will examine some important ideas propounded by these important theorists to see how they incorporated Lewin's simple, yet powerful, model of human behavior.

Bronfenbrenner's Ecological Model

Like Lewin, UrieBronfenbrenner (1979) believed that the environment plays a pivotal role in human behavior and development: "Human abilities and their realization depend in significant degree on the larger social and institutional context of individual activity" (p. xv). Bronfenbrenner based his theory of human behavior and development on the ideas of Kurt Lewin about the life space (i.e., psychological field).

However, Bronfenbrenner greatly expanded the role of the environment in human development by applying notions of systems theory, such as those of Bertalanffy (1968), to its explication. Bronfenbrenner (1979) offered a new "conception of the developing person, of the environment, and especially of the evolving interaction between the two (as) a lasting change in the way in which a person perceives and deals with his environment" (p. 3).

Bronfenbrenner defined the environment from an ecological perspective; that is, in terms of the relationship between the organism (individual) and its environment. "The ecological environment is conceived as a set of nested structures, each inside the next, like a set of Russian dolls" (Bronfenbrenner, 1979, p. 3).

According to Bronfenbrenner (1979, pp. 3–4), the inner most level (the microsystem) contains the individual and the people in the immediate surroundings (like the home and the parents); the next level (the mesosystem) consists of those systems (and the people in them) with whom the individual has frequent and important interactions (like school and teachers, or work and colleagues); a third level (the exosystem) includes people and events who influence the individual but are not, in turn, influenced by the individual (such as the workplace of the parents in the case of a child); and the final level (the macrosystem) is the culture or broader society that surrounds the individual but does not directly influence the individual on a regular basis (such as the legal system or the American way of life).

Acknowledging that his concept of the environment is "somewhat unorthodox," Bronfenbrenner (1979) nonetheless asserted that it was a necessary construct to overcome the tendency of researchers to overemphasize the personal aspects of development at the expense of the environmental impacts and the interaction between the two:

> What we find in practice, however, is a marked asymmetry, a hypertrophy of theory and research

> focusing on the properties of the person and only the most rudimentary conception and characterization of the environment in which the person is found. (p. 16)

Regardless of his reasons for developing such an elaborate model for the environment, in so doing Bronfenbrenner added a much-needed systems perspective to what is clearly a systemic problem, that of understanding the behavior and ongoing development of a human being.

Because Bronfenbrenner saw the environment, the immediate setting in which a person lives, and its supersystems, as a critical element in human development, he encapsulated his ideas into a single definition of human development which incorporates its driving forces, ongoing process, and desired outcome:

> Human development is the process through which the growing person acquires a more extended, differentiated, and valid conception of the ecological environment, and becomes motivated and able to engage in activities that reveal the properties of, sustain, or restructure that environment at levels of similar or greater complexity in form and content. (Bronfenbrenner, 1979, p. 27)

Thus, according to Bronfenbrenner (1979), to catalyze human development, change the systems in the person's environment for the better. The interaction between the person and the environment will result in an ecological transition to a higher order of human development.

For example, if you want your child to learn to read better and faster, read to him or her and make it fun. This favorable change in the microsystem (which constitutes a change in the role of the child from nonlistener to active listener and participant in the process) will encourage an ecological transition (in all likelihood the child will become motivated to learn to read on his or her own). As a result, the child will develop.

A slightly more elaborate example of Bronfenbrenner's ecological theory concerns the effect of a change in the federal laws designed to eliminate all vestiges of the glass ceiling in organizations. This macrosystem change, assuming its effective implementation, would result in workplace changes (the exosystem) that could improve the circumstances and attitude of parents, which in turn could impact the microsystem of a child positively.

If, for example, the affected parents earned a higher salary as a result of the new laws and could afford to spend more time at home with their children, the end result might be the more rapid development of each child. This effect would be directly attributable to a favorable change in the ecological environment.

Lewin argued that both personality and the environment directly affect human behavior and development [i.e., $B = f(P \cdot E)$]. Bronfenbrenner revealed the systemic role of the environment (E) in the process and thus added to our understanding of how humans develop. For a correspondingly insightful explanation of the critical role of individual personality (P) in human behavior and development, we turn to Abraham Maslow, the father of humanistic psychology.

Maslow's Hierarchy of Needs Theory

Students of management know Abraham Maslow's hierarchy of needs model. Maslow (1954/1987) postulated that human needs fall into five categories: physiological, safety, love, esteem, and self-actualization. In terms of the differences between higher and lower order needs in this hierarchy, Maslow (1954/1987) stated that:

> The basic needs arrange themselves in a fairly definite hierarchy on the basis of relative potency. Thus the safety need is stronger than the love need because it dominates the organism in various demonstrable ways when both needs are frustrated. In this sense, the physiological needs (which are themselves ordered in a subhierarchy) are stronger than the safety needs, which are stronger than the love needs, which in turn are stronger than the esteem needs, which are stronger than those idiosyncratic needs we have called the need for self-actualization. (p. 56–57).

The second part of Maslow's theory is that a satisfied need is not a motivator of behavior. This so-called "deficit principle" identifies the level a person is operating at and provides valuable clues as to what might motivate the behavior of that individual. For example, a person who is not hungry and feels safe, loved, and respected is free to self-actualize (i.e., to grow and use abilities to his or her fullest and most creative extent). Whereas, someone who feels safe and secure but not loved will persist in trying to satisfy this longing for affection, largely ignoring higher level needs in the process.

To Maslow (1954/1987), there were numerous benefits to attaining the highest order state of self-actualization, including:

1. "Living at the higher need level means greater biological efficiency, greater longevity, less disease, better sleep, appetite, and so on" (p. 57).

2. "Higher need gratifications produce more desirable subjective results, that is, more profound happiness, serenity, and richness of the inner life" (p. 57).

3. "Pursuit and gratification of higher needs present represent a general healthward trend, a trend away from psychopathology" (p. 57).

4. "The pursuit and gratification of the higher needs have desirable civic and social consequences. To some extent, the higher the need the less selfish it must be" (p. 58).

5. "The pursuit and gratification of the higher needs leads to greater, stronger, and truer individual-

> ism...People living at the level of self-actualization are, in fact, found simultaneously to love mankind most and to be the most developed idiosyncratically. This supports Fromm's contention that self-love (or better, self-respect) is synergic with rather than antagonistic to love for others" (p. 58).

In summary, Maslow believed that human development was the result of the intrinsic need, as one matures, to progress from lower level to higher level needs in search of the ultimate goal of self-actualization.

A first order examination of Maslow's theory of motivation and development in terms of the Lewinian model presented earlier suggests that Maslow did ignore [as suggested by Bronfenbrenner (1979)] the direct impact of the environment on behavior. All other things being equal, personality, as reflected in a person's operative needs, is the primary determinant of individual motivation and behavior in his hierarchy of needs theory. However, a closer examination shows that Maslow's theory does, in fact, incorporate the effect of the environment, albeit indirectly.

For example, the presence of an overt threat (such as the mugging described earlier) would create an environment characterized by a temporary concern for the lower level need of safety. Conversely, a high quality environment (which in Maslow's terms would provide for physiological, safety, and love needs at a minimum), would support the development of the higher-level ego and self-actualization needs. Hence, environment and personality do interact to determine individual behavior in Maslow's hierarchy of needs theory.

It is clear that the writings of Bronfenbrenner and Maslow provide considerable support for Lewin's simple and elegant model of human behavior and development [i.e., $B = f(P \cdot E)$]. Bolstered by this support from such renowned theorists, in the next section we use Lewin's framework as a lens through which to examine the literature of leadership and organizational change. (For more on what social scientists say about the process of human development, see Appendix A.)

Social Scientists re Leadership & Change

James MacGregor Burns (1978), in reference to the ideas of people like Lewin, Maslow, and Bronfenbrenner, stated that "vitally important, but largely unheralded work in humanistic psychology now makes it possible to generalize about leadership across cultures and across time" (p. 3). Based on his interpretation of this body of knowledge, Burns identified two forms of leadership, transactional and transforming:

> The relations of most leaders and followers are transactional—leaders approach followers with an eye to exchanging one thing for another . . . . Such transactions comprise the bulk of the relationships among leaders and followers, especially in groups . . . . Transforming leadership, while more complex, is more potent. The transforming leader recognizes and exploits an existing need or demand of a potential follower. But beyond that . . . the transforming

> leader . . . seeks to satisfy higher needs, and engages the full person of the follower. The result of transforming leadership is a relationship of mutual stimulation and elevation that converts followers into leaders and may convert leaders into moral agents . . . . (By this) I mean the kind of leadership that can produce social change that will satisfy followers' authentic needs. (Burns, 1978, p. 4)

Thus did Burns (1978) define the fundamental concept of transforming leadership—a form of leadership that is measured not in simple exchanges of rewards for services, but by its impact on its followers and society:

> Leadership is nothing if not linked to collective purpose; . . . the effectiveness of leaders must be judged not by their press clippings but by actual social change measured by intent and by the satisfaction of human needs and expectations. (Burns, 1978, p. 3)

Burns (1978) argued that transforming leaders effect change by "the satisfaction of human needs and expectations." Maslow (1954/1987) theorized that human beings develop (i.e., change and grow) by satisfying their higher level needs (i.e., self-actualizing). Hence, transforming leaders, by appealing to higher order needs, catalyze human development. Arguably, this is the fundamental reason why transforming leaders have such a powerful impact on their followers (Abrashoff, 2001; Bradford & Cohen, 1984; Bass, 1990; Senge, 1990).

In terms of Lewin's model of human behavior, by espousing a powerful, compelling vision of a "collective purpose" transforming leaders create an environment (i.e., a mesosystem, exosystem, or macrosystem) that appeals to the higher level needs of their followers. As Bronfenbrenner (1979) argued, this leads to a transition to a higher ecological state. In short, the followers develop (i.e., change) as they respond to the challenges of the new environment and work collectively to achieve the common vision (i.e., collective purpose).

Further support for the efficacy of a collaborative environment (such as that created by a transforming leader) in facilitating higher levels of follower performance and satisfaction comes from researchers in the field of organizational behavior/group management, who have extensively studied the power of collective purpose and collaborative effort to catalyze human action (Johnson & Johnson, 1989, p. 169).

To summarize the results of this body of accumulated knowledge related to the issue of collaboration, Johnson and Johnson (1989) conducted aggregate analyses of these primary research findings. Johnson and Johnson (1989) described the findings of their meta-analytic research of over 500 hundred such studies as follows:

> On the basis of the research to date (which is considerable), it may be concluded that generally achievement and productivity were higher in cooperative situations than in competitive or individualistic ones, and that cooperative efforts resulted in more frequent use of higher-level reasoning strate-

> gies, more frequent generation of new ideas and solutions (i.e., process gains), and greater transfer of learning (i.e., greater productivity on subsequent similar tasks done individually) than did competitive and individualistic efforts. (p. 171)

Corroboration of these empirical research findings comes from Abrashoff (2001), who described a practical application of transforming leadership that demonstrated the inherent power of a cooperative, supportive environment (compared to a competitive, individualistic one) to effect meaningful, lasting organizational change. Captain Abrashoff took over as commander of the US Benfold, a fighting ship in the modern navy that was plagued by extremely low morale and very high turnover.

According to Abrashoff (2001), "the Benfold's 310 sailors were so unhappy with their lives on board they literally cheered when my predecessor left the shift for the last time. I vowed that would never happen to me" (p. 139). Captain Abrashoff used the principles of transforming leadership to engineer a remarkable turnaround. By "rejecting the 225-year-old U.S. Navy way of running things" (Abrashoff, 2001, p. 138) (i.e., the top-down, command-and-control leadership style) and replacing it with a collaborative, supportive style, Captain Abrashoff reached the men and motivated them to work together to ensure that the proper functioning of the ship. "Today, the vessel is the pride of the Pacific fleet, and sailors from other ships are clamoring to join its crew" (Abrashoff, 2001, p. 138).

So far, Kurt Lewin's model of behavior has proven effective as a lens through which to view the essence of leadership and change; enabling us to interpret important theory, research, and practice related to modern, transforming leadership. Another of Lewin's models, one that incorporates his behavioral model and describes the fundamental nature of change, will enable us to bridge the gap between the fields of leadership and change to achieve the creative synthesis we desire.

Integrating Leadership & Change

Organizational change is the flip side of the leadership coin. Without purposive leadership, change is haphazard, reactive, and transitory. With transforming leadership, it is planned, proactive, and effective.

As discussed in Appendix B, major schools of leadership theory have focused on the traits, behavior, situational responses, and charisma of the leader, respectively (Daft, 1999). However, proponents of planned change have examined leadership in terms of the crucial role of the leader as a change agent (Jaffe & Scott, 2000; Kalagher, 2002; Kotter, 1996). Surprisingly little literature has focused on the integration of the theories and research in these two important, complementary domains of human knowledge. The goal of this section is to propose a mechanism for such a synthesis.

To integrate leadership and change, it is important to decide which comes first. The preponderance of literature assumes that leadership is multi-faceted, and that only one of these facets is change management (i.e., enablement). While this view is hardly contentious, what is required for a creative synthesis is a shift to the perspective that transformation (i.e., major change) is the essential function of modern leadership, and that all other aspects of leadership support this primary focus.

As we have seen, many have already recognized that the realities of the information age demand such a new style of leadership; one that embraces transformation as the goal of organizational and societal change and views the change effort as a collaborative undertaking between leaders and followers at all levels (Abrashoff, 2001; Abshire, 2001; Ackoff, 1999; Bennis, 1999; Burns, 1978). Once again, Kurt Lewin, the principal architect of many of the most powerful theories in modern change management and organization development (Burke, 1982; Marrow, 1969; Schein, 1999), provides a framework that meets our need.

Kurt Lewin's Change Model

One of the most important of Lewin's theories is the simple and elegant three-step change model consisting of (a) unfreezing, (b) movement (i.e., change), and (c) refreezing (Burke, 1987).

> The first step in the process of change is unfreezing the present level of behavior . . . . The second step, movement, is to take action that will change the social system from its original level of behavior or operation to a new level . . . . The refreezing step involves the establishment of a process that will

> make the new level of behavior "relatively secure against change." (Burke, 1987, pp. 54–56)

As we have seen in chapter 2, strong support for the validity of Lewin's change model as a framework for understanding leadership and organizational change comes from Elrod and Tippett (2002), who compared 15 change models from the literatures of personal development and of organizational change.

> The majority (13 out of 15) of these "change models" transition from normality through some form of disruption and then to a re-defined normality. In the initial state of normality, a reasonable level of performance can be maintained. However, an individual, or an organization passes through the region of disruption, performance can be expected to be diminished. In the final state, a re-defined normality, the understandings and perspectives of the changed entity (individual or organization) are more closely aligned with reality and performance increases. (Elrod and Tippett, 2002, p. 285)

Based on the evidence presented, it is clear that Lewin's change model provides an excellent basis for a model of leadership and organizational change. In effect, Lewin urges the modern, would-be-transforming leader to unfreeze the current environment, encourage movement or change to a new state, and refreeze the environment so that the new state permanently replaces the old state.

An Integrative L & C Model

To implement the first step in Lewin's change process, a leader begins by unfreezing the current situation (i.e., the current state) to overcome inherent resistance to change. Leaders do this in one of two ways. Traditional, command-and-control leaders either point to an existing, survival-threatening crisis that demands immediate action or, in cases where there is no real crisis, manufacture one to compel their subordinates to take action (Kotter, 1996). Transforming leaders unfreeze a situation by creating a vision of the future and encouraging and empowering the members of the organization to work together to make it a reality (Abrashoff, 2001; Burns, 1978, 2003; Senge, 1990).

Change occurs in the second (movement) phase. The movement of the system can result from an intervention aimed at the individual, group, organizational, or higher level (Burke, 1982). According to Burke (1982), management training and job redesign are typical individual-level interventions; team building is the most popular group-level intervention; and process reengineering and total quality management are examples of interventions aimed at organization-wide change.

In this second step, the leader once again has important decisions to make that can derail, delay, or accelerate the change process. Traditional leaders often decide unilaterally what is good for the individual, group, or organization and impose top-down solutions to perceived organizational problems. For example, command-and-control managers often mandate training for specific individuals as the solution to problems caused by systemic forces (such as non-aligned organization structure, inadequate reward systems, bad management, etc.) which are actually beyond the control of any one individual.

Transforming leaders avoid these misguided, top-down interventions, except in those rare cases when immediate, unilateral action is necessary to avert a crisis. Rather, they take the time to engage the members of the organization in a collaborative, third-party facilitated change effort based on vision, enrollment, alignment, joint problem identification, collaborative problem solving, mutual support throughout the change process, and joint evaluation and re-visioning (Bennis, 1999; Bradford & Cohen, 1984; Burke, 1987; Senge, 1990).

When the time comes to refreeze (i.e., institutionalize) the changes, once again the difference between transforming leaders and traditional managers is noteworthy. Top-down leaders often direct and expect organization members affected by the change to follow the new procedures, systems, or policies without question; thus, mistaking change for transition (Bridges, 1980, 1991) and engendering further resistance. Transforming leaders, having secured buy-in at each stage of the change process, focus their efforts on developing the capability of the organization's members and ensuring a high level of organizational learning from the change process. In this way, they enable their followers to manifest the attitudes and actions necessary to ensure the relative permanence of and payoffs from the new system, while instilling a readiness to change the new system if required (Bradford & Cohen, 1984; Burke, 1987; Senge, 1990). Finally, when necessary to meet the demands of a rapidly changing environment (Bennis, 1999), transforming leaders facilitate a new round of proactive change based on the three-step Lewin model.

The aggregate effect of applying this modern leadership model is the creation of an environment that stimulates a change in behavior and movement toward the fulfillment of higher order needs through the attainment of the common vision. Thus, the modern leadership and change model subsumes both Lewin's change and behavior models. Furthermore, it incorporates ideas and insights suggested by the work of many important social scientists. Finally, it incorporates the four elements of the new transformative change paradigm–it is systemic, transformative, integrative, and collaborative.

Conclusion

We began this chapter with the goal of synthesizing from the work of theorists, researchers, and practitioners a leadership and change model that would incorporate the elements of the new paradigm for transformative change and guide modern leaders in a step-by-step fashion through the process of catalyzing and managing extraordinary change.

We discovered that modern leaders transform their organizations and society to meet the demands of their evolving environments by (a) engaging their followers in the creation of a compelling, systemic, shared vision of the future, (b) by sharing responsibility (and authority) with their followers for developing and implementing joint action plans to achieve that collective purpose, and (c) by focusing on the development and learning of the organization, its groups/teams and members, to enable them to implement and sustain the changes needed to achieve the vision.

To remember this three-stage leadership and change model, think of it in these simple terms. Modern leaders do three key things to enable transformative change:

1. Create a shared, systemic vision to initiate it.
2. Facilitate an integrative, collaborative process to achieve it.
3. Enable ongoing, systemic development/learning to sustain it.

As modern leaders, when we apply this three-stage process, we are implicitly guided by the four elements or principles of the new paradigm for transformative change which it encompasses:

- A Systemic World View
- A Transformative Vision
- An Integrative Scholarship
- A Collaborative Process

Equipped with this scientific knowledge about leadership and change, we are theoretically ready to tackle problems of great import to individuals, groups, organizations, and society as a whole in the 21st century. In the next part of the book, we examine some practical ways to increase the odds of doing this successfully.

Part II

The 21st Century Leader in Action

Chapter 4

The Modern Leadership Model

How do you lead? Do you plan, organize, staff, exert influence, and control? Or is that the definition of management? Do you focus on providing strategic direction and leave the implementation to others? Or do you dive into the details of day-to-day operations to ensure that people do things right? Do you one-minute manage or do you focus on moving the cheese?

Decisions, Decisions, Decisions!

Based on the insights about effective leadership gained in the first part of this book, you know that the answer is a resounding "None of the above." In fact, the answer lies in a creative synthesis of time-honored management practices, contemporary leadership principles, and a few secret ingredients from the experts in change management.

A Creative Synthesis

Kurt Lewin's famous three-stage model of change—unfreezing, movement, and refreezing—is the starting point in our design process (Burke, 1987). To reinforce the primacy of Lewin's ingenious solution to the basic problem of systemic change (be it individual growth, team development, organizational change, or societal transformation) our modern leadership model has three basic parts, not two, four, seven or any other number.

Unfreezing by Visionary Direction Setting

Lewin provided us with yet another key element for the modern leadership model. Namely, that unfreezing should be a positive process aimed at engaging the members of the system in the change process, not a negative one aimed at coercing their participation. Hence, the first stage in the model begins with the creation of a powerful, compelling vision of a future that excites, energizes, and engages everybody involved in the change effort. As we will see in the next chapter, leaders do not accomplish this in isolation, but together with their followers.

Movement by Action Research Implementation

Once the "collective purpose" or common vision of the future is in place, a plan to get from the current state of affairs to the desired future state is necessary. Here, the traditional concept of planning has its day, but not in the old fashioned, top-down manner often associated with a formal planning process. In its place, is a participative, third-party led, action research intervention designed to engage the major stakeholders in a collaborative process for deciding how to bridge the gap between the current reality and the common vision of an ideal future state. The result of this process is both a plan of action and a highly motivated, empowered set of participants.

A collaborative, team-based effort, led by empowered members of the system highly motivated to implement the joint action plans and change strategies accelerates the movement phase of the process. In practice, this resembles the operation of a championship team or a symphony orchestra in that people work together, regardless of position, to achieve the common vision. Team members and leaders mutually agree to and jointly monitor progress against project goals. Since they view the need for corrective action as integral to the process and not cause for blame, team members take corrective action jointly and swiftly to keep the mission on course. If the team agrees that a team member needs to learn a new set of skills to enable the team to move ahead, the team, with the consent of the leader, authorizes the necessary training or development. In short, team members work together with leadership to get the job done.

Refreezing by System Development and Learning

The final step in the modern leadership model involves the institutionalization of changes made to achieve the vision. This consists of two types of initiatives: those that focus on improving the current functioning of the overall system (i.e., system development) and those that focus on enhancing its future effectiveness (i.e., system learning).

System development efforts focus on improving system effectiveness by implementing throughout the system the new methods created during the change process. In effect, they enable the members of the system to become better at their current work. On the other hand, system learning efforts try to answer the question, "Is there a better way to do this in the future?"

As we shall see later, there are many techniques for refreezing a situation after a major change effort. They include traditional methods, such as individual training and development and organization development (Burke, 1982), as well as more contemporary approaches, such as organizational learning (Senge, 1990) and knowledge management (Cavaleri, Seivert, & Lee, 2005; Wiig, 2004).

Summary

The modern leadership model is by design a simple and, hopefully, elegant three-part process, grounded in the theories and research findings of experts in the field of leadership and change, which any transforming leader can apply to enable substantive change. These steps are:

Stage	Purpose	Description
1	Unfreezing	Visionary Direction Setting
2	Movement	Action Research Intervention
3	Refreezing	System Development/Learning

In the remaining sections of this chapter, we explore some key principles that can guide leaders as they apply each stage of the modern leadership model in the implementation of transformative, systemic change at the individual, team, organizational, or societal level.

Stage 1—Visionary Direction Setting

Setting the strategic direction for a system, such as a group or organization, is unquestionably one of the primary responsibilities of a leader. There are three basic ways to do it. One is simply to decide on the new direction, communicate it, and answer questions about it. Another is to let external forces set the direction for you. A third is to create an initial vision of an ideal future state and share it with your followers. This you do by engaging your followers in an interactive process that allows them to work with you to enhance your vision with their ideas, hopes, and dreams until it becomes a shared/common vision, a "collective purpose," that all are committed to achieving.

In terms of unfreezing, the difference between the third way and the first two is, to paraphrase Mark Twain again, like the difference between lightning and the lightning bug. Let us examine the chain of events set in motion by each direction setting method to see why.

Top-Down Direction Setting

If you "take charge" and decide on a strategic direction unilaterally, you confront your followers with the need to change essentially because you say so. The knee-jerk reaction of most people to any directive, unless they have little or no choice, is to resist. When perceived by a top-down leader, this resistance to change typically engenders a strong and immediate response; namely, the leader plays the "I'm the boss" card.

This increase in the pressure to change elicits an even stronger resistance from many of the followers, whether they appear to acquiesce or not. Even if the leader achieves his or her goal of coercing acceptance of the new direction, it generally comes at the cost of lowered productivity and morale, measured in a plethora of undesirable ways, such as unnecessary delays, lack of commitment, passive aggressive behavior, and, on occasion, overt confrontation. Regardless of the form taken by the resistance to change, it is not positive.

External Direction Setting

Some leaders prefer not to set the course. They simply let external forces shape their destiny. If you allow the environment to set the strategic direction, you run two risks. First, your failure to take proactive measures to deal with the external threats and opportunities may force you to play catch up, which could threaten your survival. Second, when you finally react to the crises created by these external forces, you will strain your people to the limit and incur their ire for your laissez-faire leadership style.

Although a crisis will almost certainly promote some movement in the direction of resolving it, which is what you want, your followers will be unhappy, which is something that you don't want. Often, negative factors associated with the new direction will diminish their willingness to accept it. These factors could include feeling overworked, overstressed, and victimized by an ineffective leadership that doesn't do its job of scanning the environment and developing plans for dealing with potentially negative situations before they get out of hand. In short, reacting to external forces is also a negative way to unfreeze the system.

Visionary Direction Setting

To be a visionary it is not sufficient to have a vision. You must share that vision with others and engage them in a process of refining or enhancing it so that the resulting shared vision speaks to them as well as you. It is this collaborative interaction between leader and follower that spawn's the "collective purpose" that Burns (1978) saw as the overarching goal of the transforming leader.

Because it resonates with their goals and promises to satisfy their higher level human needs, a creative, compelling, concrete vision of an ideal future state has the power to unfreeze a situation dramatically. We all know how President John F. Kennedy's vision of an American walking on the moon catalyzed NASA and the country in the nineteen sixties.

Your goal, as a leader, is to facilitate a participative process that engages your followers in the creation of an equally compelling vision, albeit on a smaller scale; one that energizes, excites, and empowers them, like you, to take the actions needed to make it a reality.

Before discussing the essential role of collaborative action planning in creating the blue print for system change and catalyzing movement toward the shared vision, we need to examine briefly some issues that occasionally frustrate people's efforts to achieve a common vision.

Mission or Vision: Which Comes First?

Do not fall into the trap of worrying about the minor differences between vision and mission, or vision and any other seemingly related concept, like overarching goal, objective, etc. Semantics should not prevent you and your followers from developing a truly powerful description of the end state you desire to achieve. In the words of the bard, "What's in a name? That which we call a rose by any other word would smell as sweet" (Shakespeare, 1960, p. 39).

If the Shoe Doesn't Fit, Don't Wear It

People are smart, especially the people you interact with every day. So, if this strikes you as some version of the "vision thing," it is definitely not for you. Visionary direction setting is not the latest fad, nor is it outdated. It is a proven method for motivating groups of people to take collective action to achieve shared goals. However, involvement in a participative process tests leaders in ways that conventional processes, like delegation, do not. Sharing power amicably and equitably is not easy. But, when done well, it produces enormous rewards for all concerned. It is the hallmark of the 21st century leader.

Summary

You will promote the positive unfreezing that you desire if you engage the members of the system in a participative process for creating a shared vision of an ideal future. Then, as we will see in the next section, you will catalyze movement toward that "collective purpose" by engaging people in a collaborative process for developing and implementing joint action plans for achieving that vision.

Stage 2—Action Research Intervention

Vision and planning are two sides of the same coin. Without vision, we have no desired outcome; no ideal future state; no overarching goal; no collective purpose; no strategic direction. Without planning, we have the promise of a bright future, but no means of attaining it.

Fortunately, as the leader, you do not have to figure out how to manifest or attain the shared vision by yourself. In fact, you must resist the temptation to do so. Your choice to facilitate a process for creating a common vision is a de facto commitment to a collaborative change process of visioning, action planning and implementation, and refreezing. Your followers, having engaged in a participatory visioning process, will expect to play an active role in the rest of the change process. As a wise leader, you would not want it any other way.

If you have qualms about this level of involvement in the process by the members of your organization, take solace in the fact that many other leaders have successfully surmounted the issues faced by groups when working in a collaborative process to achieve a common goal. In fact, experience has shown that a correctly facilitated, participative process results in (a) dramatically higher productivity and morale during the change effort, and (b) a much higher probability of achieving the desired outcomes (Abrashoff, 2001; Bradford & Cohen, 1984; Weisbord & Janoff, 1995).

To maximize the probability of manifesting the vision, the transforming leader engages and works collaboratively with experts in organization development and change enablement. These third-party change agents bring the needed objectivity and expertise to the effort and are essential to its success. Leaders who rely on in-house staff experts known to the participants run the risk of (a) alienating their followers (who often view the staff as biased) and, thus, unwittingly increasing resistance to change; (b) not getting the desired results due to unresolved group issues that interfere with team efforts; or (c) not getting the desired outcomes because staff lack the expertise to facilitate the change effort properly.

Think of this choice as the difference between trying to diagnose and cure what ails you by yourself, versus seeking out competent medical help for the treatment of a serious condition. Alternatively, think of it as trying to build your dream house without engaging an architect to design it first. In either case, you might succeed on your own, but it is probably not worth the risk.

An essential characteristic of a collaborative change intervention is its reliance on Kurt Lewin's action research model (Burke, 1982, p. 8). The method has two phases. The first or research phase involves collecting data on problems, analyzing that data, and designing corrective measures based on the analysis. The second or action phase involves implementing these action plans within the system. Observation and further data analysis (research) may suggest the need for further action. This ongoing cycle of action based on research and research based on action is what Lewin called action research.

The connection between the common visioning of the unfreezing stage and the joint action research intervention of the movement stage is a crucial one. Simply put, the broad directional objectives developed in visionary direction setting are really more like vision elements (component parts of the vision) than implementable plans. Due to their high level, strategic nature, they are not detailed or grounded enough to serve as the basis for intervening in the day-today operations of the system to effect positive change. This is where action research comes into play.

In practice, the action research process entails the following related steps: (a) the collection of data from the members of the system, (b) preliminary analysis of the data, (c) presentation of the data and tentative findings to the participants in the change effort, (d) joint agreement on the problems and priorities, and (e) joint determination of what to do to achieve the vision or vision elements. Then, teams committed to manifesting elements of the vision (f) develop detailed action plans (i.e., intervention strategies) and implement them within the system.

As these teams work, they routinely report their progress to leadership and to the other teams engaged in the change to ensure that the process converges on the desired outcome(s) in a timely and effective manner. This high level of involvement in project planning and implementation by all of the participants is crucial to the success of a collaborative change process.

What is striking about these team efforts is the high level of energy and commitment of the team members. There are at least three reasons for this phenomenon. First, it is partly due to the empowering effect of being involved in an important, vision-driven, collaborative change effort.

Second, the fact that leaders do not assign team members to teams in an action-research intervention is also a major factor. Because participants select the projects they want most to work on, they feel a higher degree of responsibility for making their project a success, and derive a higher level of satisfaction from participating in a joint effort to attain the goals of the project.

Finally, because leadership empowers the third party change agents to facilitate the development of the teams into autonomous units, much like the self-directed teams that build an entire automobile in a modern manufacturing plant, team members feel that they and their contributions are important to the success of the entire organization.

The primary role of the modern leader is to facilitate the overall change process. So, in addition to communicating what you are doing to stakeholders, you must be present and actively engaged at many key points in the process. Remember, this is a collaborative undertaking involving you and your followers. So, you must not only observe the process, but also actively participate in it. Later, when we explore the anatomy of an intervention in more detail, we will identify some key points in the change effort and examine your role at these pivotal moments. First, however, we complete our overview of the modern leadership model by exploring the final, refreezing stage.

Stage 3—System Development/Learning

Did the change effort succeed? Whether the answer to this question is yes, or no, your next step is clear if you are a believer in learning from your experiences. You ensure that the lessons learned from the change are shared with the others in the system to (a) develop their capability to use the new ideas and approaches created in the action research phase (system development) and (b) foster deeper thinking about ways to enhance system performance even more (system learning). The overall effect of this knowledge transfer is to refreeze the system into a new, more effective, configuration while ensuring its ability to respond and adapt to new environmental threats and opportunities.

There are many traditional methods for making this knowledge transfer happen. Training is a popular way of passing on vital information about some new method and developing the skills required to apply it. For example, in business process reengineering, people who will use the newly redesigned process will need training about how it works. Formal changes in policies and procedures, and the institution of team-based rewards as a component of compensation for team efforts, are other traditional ways of ensuring system development and the institutionalization of change.

Capturing and reflecting collectively on the lessons learned from a change effort is a powerful method of simultaneously institutionalizing the changes and avoiding complacency. At the core of system learning (i.e., individual, team, and organizational learning) is the conviction that critical thinking about successes and failures leads directly to system improvement.

Proponents of some form of organizational learning have long touted the benefits to organizations of engaging in substantive dialogue about the true meaning of important lessons learned from change (Argyris & Schon, 1978; Senge, 1990). In addition, the current wave of new, technology-based initiatives in knowledge and learning management holds great promise for assisting insightful modern leaders in their efforts to mine their systems' collective knowledge (Cavaleri, Seivert, & Lee, 2005; Wiig, 2004).

In the next chapter, we will examine how to apply the principles and practices of modern leadership to effect positive social change. Since systemic change affects all of the components of the system, we will explore the anatomy of a collaborative change effort designed to change individuals, groups, and the whole organization simultaneously.

Chapter 5

Anatomy of a Transformative Change

Systemic interventions occur on multiple levels simultaneously. An effort to transform an organization, for example, affects each component of the system—the individual members, the groups to which the members belong, the organization as a whole, and its environment. It is important to address each of these levels to ensure the success of the overall change effort. Neglecting one or more could lead to failure. While this makes change enablement more difficult, it also increases the odds of effecting meaningful, lasting change if done correctly.

To demonstrate how a leader/change agent who is cognizant of the systemic nature of change would apply the principles of modern leadership to effect an organizational transformation, we will focus in this chapter on a concrete, albeit hypothetical, situation. Specifically, we will explore a change effort precipitated by the need for an organization in a dynamic, competitive market to transform itself from a product-focus to a customer-focus to serve its customers better and, thereby, ensure its survival.

Visionary Direction Setting

Experts in change management know that implementation begins on the first day of a change effort, and that it begins with the leader. After all, you can't expect your followers to do what you aren't willing to do. This willingness to change, with a goal of personal mastery, is one of the core competencies or disciplines of the modern leader (Senge, 1990). For example, if you want the people in your organization to work together (i.e., collaborate) to get things done, you have to learn to manage in a participative manner. This may be your first real test, especially if you have been successful in the past as an authoritarian leader. But, you must embrace the opportunity to work with the people you would lead in the transformative change process or you will send a mixed message from the outset (i.e., "Do as I say, not as I do."), and interfere with the change process. After all, who wants to follow a leader who lacks integrity?

Most leaders are familiar with the classic leadership style continuum (first articulated by Kurt Lewin) that ranges from autocratic, top-down, command-and-control, directive, "I'm the Boss" leadership on the one hand to democratic, collaborative, participative, "We're in this together" leadership on the other. The personal journey from authoritative to collaborative, which is usually born out of necessity, is one that many leaders undertake with great trepidation.

The biggest fear of most traditional leaders is that, if they share responsibility with their followers, they will lose control at some point in the process. They assume that the more responsibility and authority they share with their followers, the less control they will have over the outcomes, as if leadership were a zero-sum game.

The reality of a truly collaborative process is that the people who are committed to achieving the goals of a transformative change will take responsibility for achieving those shared outcomes. Once leaders experience the paradoxical increase in control that results from sharing power in a collaborative process, they happily stop resisting and turn their attention to other important aspects of their jobs.

Personal Vision

Assuming that you are at the point where you are ready to launch and fully participate in a collaborative, transformative change effort, what is the first thing that you must do? The answer is simple. The modern leadership model says that vision comes first. So you must start by developing your view of the ideal future state and sharing it with others.

To help you do this, imagine that your change management consultant asks you this question: "If you could have exactly what you want for your organization and its customers in the future, what would it be?" Noticing that this question does not bound your answer in any way, you feel free to imagine an ideal scenario. What you arrive at is a vision that speaks of an organization of concerned, committed, and empowered professionals attuned to each customer's unique needs, whose customers recognize and reward them for providing the best products, services, and customer service in the industry.

Common Vision

You write your vision down, and then begin communicating and discussing it with your followers in a set of dialogues designed to elicit the meaning of your vision and its potential impact on the organization and each person in it. While not ignoring questions from naysayers troubled by and mired in the reality of the current state, you do not permit them to stop or unduly delay the change process or to dampen the enthusiasm of others who see the need for change as essential to survival and are, therefore, ready to take on the challenge of transforming their organization. Instead, you ask everyone to suspend judgment temporarily and imagine themselves as full participants in the new organization.

As a result of this interactive process of sharing your vision with the members of the organization and engaging them in a dialogue about its personal and professional meaning, an enhanced vision for the future of your organization emerges, one that you and your followers share. This shared or common vision is your "collective purpose."

As you discuss this exciting vision of an ideal future with the members of your organization, you make a point of explaining your commitment to working with them in a collaborative process to effect this crucial transformation. You explain that, under your direction and with your full support, third-party consultants will facilitate a participative change process that will begin with the collection, analysis, and feedback of data about current issues and concerns. Once reviewed, enhanced, and agreed upon by consensus of the members of the organization participating, this collective knowledge will inform the process of creating the organizational structures, processes, systems, and policies needed to support a transformed organization.

Action Research Intervention

You commission the third party consultants to interview key people in the organization on a confidential basis to collect data on the current state. Simultaneously, you announce a work conference at which the entire organization or a representative cross-section of members (if the organization is too large to meet in one place), including those who participate in these interviews, will review the data, distill its key messages, and develop preliminary action plans to resolve the issues in accordance with the common vision.

Early in the conference, all of the members of the collaborative work conference produce a list of prioritized issues using the nominal group technique or a similar consensus building process. Then, groups of self-selected participants focus on each of the major issues. During the conference, these groups develop joint (i.e., collaborative) action plans to address their issues and share their tentative analyzes and findings with the entire group. Based on the feedback they receive, the groups revise their action plans.

After the conference, the groups work together to put their approved action plans into action. During this period, third-party consultants work with the groups to build them into high-performance teams and facilitate their work. Each group either reengineers existing processes or develops prototypes for completely new systems or processes. To ensure a smooth implementation or phasing in of these modified or new approaches, third-party consultants assist each team in developing an implementation strategy which considers the needs of those whose work the modified/new systems will impact.

System Development and Learning

After the movement phase has taken place, refreezing is necessary. To this end, the modern organizational leader focuses on individual, group, organizational, and system development. The type of interventions (with the corresponding system levels they address in parentheses) a leader might use to institutionalize the new methods and behaviors in a system include (individual) training and development, (team) building, (organizational) development, and direct interaction with parts of the organization's (external environment) to educate them or otherwise improve their relationship with the organization.

If a post-change dialogue among the change agents, change participants, and stakeholders affected by the change also reveals external threats to the system or opportunities, then the leader authorizes appropriate interventions aimed at discovering new approaches and ideas that will enable the organization to thwart these external threats or capitalize on the opportunities.

Thus, the system development activity associated with a change effort informs a larger, organizational-level, "double-loop" learning initiative (Argyris & Schon, 1978) that focuses on a deeper, ongoing examination of environmental factors —political, social, technological, natural, legal, governmental, and competitive trends— and what the organization must do to optimize its competitive position in the future in light of these factors. Recognizing the importance of continuous dialogue on the subject to the organization, the modern, transformative leader champions this systemic learning activity; thus ensuring that it is ongoing and informed by the lessons learned from individual change efforts.

The System Change Matrix

To help you envision what goes on during a systemic intervention, imagine each of the levels of a system (i.e., individual, group/team, organization, and environment) as rows in a matrix or table, and each of the phases of the change process (i.e., unfreezing, movement, refreezing) as columns. During an intervention, things might be happening simultaneously at any or all of these levels.

As time progresses, movement generally occurs from left to right, i.e., from unfreezing to refreezing. Since change at any level is an iterative rather than a linear process, it may, however, be necessary to cycle back to an earlier stage to adjust something that isn't working quite right.

For example, if you inadvertently forget to inform certain key stakeholders of your intervention into the system, you may have to go back to phase one to involve them in the process before proceeding. Alternatively, if you realize that you have left key system members off the list of work conference participants, you may have to invite them and adjust your arrangements and conference design accordingly. Similarly, if you failed to include in the change process a group who are essential to the system-wide institutionalization of the new methods, you may have to initiate an intervention designed to bring them on board, even at the eleventh hour.

Although an actual change diagram for a systemic intervention will be more complicated, a schematic representation of the change matrix in our hypothetical example looks like this:

Level	**Unfreezing**	**Movement**	**Refreezing**
Environment	2	3	1
Organization	2	2	1
Group/Team	2	1	1
Individual	1	2	1

The numbers in the cells indicate focus. For example, the individual is the primary focus during the initial, unfreezing stage. The leader initiates this stage by creating a concrete, compelling vision of the future. He or she then informs and engages key external stakeholders to get their buy-in and support for the change. The leader then engages individuals in the organization, regardless of their group or team membership, in an interactive dialogue whose purpose is to develop a common vision for the part of the system that will undergo the change. As stated, the focus of this effort is largely on the individuals in the system.

During the movement phase, the self-selected, high energy teams responsible for creating the new methods become the primary focus. Individuals in the organization who are not involved in the change process, but whom the change will impact, receive regular progress reports to keep them (a) in the loop about the details of the change effort and (b) motivated to see it through. External (to the organization) stakeholders, who are interested but further removed from the change, receive less frequent, higher level feedback on progress.

During the refreezing phase, all levels are theoretically important. Proper closure requires system development and learning of the type described earlier. The exact nature of the knowledge/learning management and system development interventions needed becomes clear as a result of the dialogue that takes place among system members during this final, refreezing phase of the change effort. The focus emerges from the shared dialogue.

Conclusion

In this chapter, we have examined some of the critical success factors for any transformative change effort and presented a systemic change matrix which captures the essence of the change process and focuses attention on "doing the right thing" at the right stage of the process.

In the next chapter, we will examine how modern leaders might use this transformative change process to address important problems in the 21st century.

Chapter 6

21st Century Leadership & Change

Dialogue! Dialogue! Dialogue! The search for understanding and shared meaning that begins with the curiosity to ask and a willingness to listen is the key to leadership and change in the 21st century.

Traditional communication methods, such as discussion, (which, in practice, often resembles percussion, i.e., the delivery a sharp blow), and debate (which is typically discussion on steroids), are means of human interaction based on a win-lose mentality. They have no place in the search for the truth and fair solutions to complex personal, team, organizational, and societal problems in the global village.

Instead, we must (re)discover methods of interacting that support win-win solutions to our most pressing common problems. Given our increasing planetary interdependence, it makes senses to look for dialogue-based leadership and change models that have served others who needed to collaborate in the past effectively. Here are a few examples that come to mind.

A jury faced with convicting someone of murder must make a collaborative decision. All twelve must agree on the verdict. As a result, their interactions focus on the search for the truth and a consensus that they have ascertained it. Although jury deliberations often begin as debates or discussions, when they work, they eventually transform into the dialogue necessary to ensure a just verdict. Anyone who has served on a jury that worked understands the true nature of consensus decision-making and its power to arrive at a fair verdict.

Nomadic tribes faced with the need to survive and requiring the efforts of every able-bodied member to do it understand the need for collaborative decision-making and cooperative effort. Decisions affecting life and death, such as when to move, are tribal decisions. The tribe seeks the wisdom of all and applies it to arrive at the best decision.

As discussed in chapter 3, meta-analytic research by Johnson and Johnson (1989) demonstrated quantitatively the superiority of cooperative decision making over individualistic, competitive decision making. In the majority of situations, group performance and member satisfaction are both higher when the leader creates a cooperative climate for problem solving and decision making.

Game theory shows that, even in a zero-sum game, joint or collaborative action yields a higher payoff (a win-win) than individualistic, competitive action—the highest possible payoff in fact. For example, we all know from watching crime shows on TV that if two people suspected of a crime trust each other enough not to cave in and accuse each other of the crime when interrogated separately by the police, they both go free. Knowing this, the police promise each suspect either immunity or a reduced sentence in return for testimony against the other. Usually this works and self-interest wins out over group interest, but sometimes the trust level is high enough that neither suspect turns state's evidence, so both are set free.

If you think that this is a bad outcome for society and, therefore, find it hard to appreciate the value of this example as an illustration of the effectiveness of collaborative behavior in interdependent situations, consider how you would feel if you and your spouse were the ones falsely accused of the crime.

Organization Development (OD) consultants and other change management experts have used collaborative processes for years to effect positive social change at the group, organization, and societal level (Burke, 1982; Weisbord & Janoff, 1995).

Based on this strong evidence of the efficacy of collaborative effort in effecting change, the first step of every would-be transforming leader in the modern era is clear: Bring together those who have a stake in the solution of a problem or the pursuit of an opportunity, and engage in a dialogue aimed at developing insight into the real interests of the parties involved, not their initial positions. The common interest which will form the basis for a meaningful collaborative solution will emerge from this dialogue.

After Dialogue, What Happens Next?

The short answer to this question is that you apply the modern leadership model. As a group, you are steeped in shared meaning and collective intent as a result of a collaborative dialogue aimed at finding common ground. Your next steps are, therefore, to:

1. Create a shared, systemic vision of the future.

2. Facilitate an integrative, collaborative process.

3. Enable ongoing, systemic development/learning.

Remember that this approach incorporates the four principles of the new paradigm for transformative change which it encompasses:

- A Systemic World View
- A Transformative Vision
- An Integrative Scholarship
- A Collaborative Process

Equipped with theoretical knowledge (from Part I) and practical insight (from Part II) about leadership and change, you are now ready to tackle problems of great import to individuals, groups, organizations, and society as a whole in the 21st century. We wish you well.

Part III

Appendixes

A Principles of Human Development

B Leadership Theories

C OD & Change Management

Appendix A

Principles of Human Development

What are the principles of human development? How do they support the transformative leadership and change concepts incorporated in the modern leadership model?

To answer these questions, in this essay we examine important classic and contemporary theories of human development, such as those of Maslow, Erikson, Kegan, and Bronfenbrenner, and attempt to synthesize them into a coherent set of essential characteristics for any contemporary model of leadership and development.

Table of Contents

Nature of Human Development

According to the biographer, Marrow (1969), Kurt Lewin, the famous psychologist who developed the basic concepts of group dynamics, action research, field theory, and sensitivity training, once said, "There is nothing so practical as a good theory" (p. viii). So, to understand the nature of human development, it is important to have some prior theory. Lewin himself provided just such a simple and useful model of human development, which will serve as a lens for interpreting the theories of human development presented in this essay.

According to Marrow (1969), Lewin believed that "the behavior of a person can be predicted — but only if his *total* psychological field or life space at a given moment is known" (p. 59). Regarding the life space, Lewin maintained that applications of field theory were possible in all branches of psychology. He viewed the life space as the psychologist's universe. In it, person and environment are interrelated and individual behavior is always derived from the relation of the concrete individual to the concrete situation. Behavior, therefore, is a function of the life space: B = f (LS), which in turn is a product of the interaction between the person, P, and his (or her) environment, E. (Marrow, 1969, p. 38)

Building on these life space variables as postulated by Lewin, the human development model rests on two primary constructs. First, if the behavior of an individual changes from one observation (point in time) to another (at a later time), the resulting delta or difference in behavior is an indication of possible growth (development). Such an observable difference in behavior is a necessary, but not sufficient, condition for growth. Second, the observed difference in behavior must meet the following conditions:

1. It must last or persist for some time.

2. It must represent an improvement in behavior.

3. It must be due primarily to a change in the person (P), not the environment (E).

Taken together these requirements represent necessary and sufficient evidence of human development.

To clarify these constructs, consider how the model classifies behavior in a few simple examples. First, imagine a case where a change is temporary, such as when a child behaves just long enough to get the candy it wants then reverts to spontaneous and unmotivated (by the external environment) outbursts. This change in behavior, while observable, clearly violates the persistence condition (i.e., it does not last) and, hence, is not true development.

Second, imagine a case where a bad behavior gets worse over time. This observable change represents degradation in performance and is the opposite of growth/development.

Third, imagine a case where an observable difference in behavior is entirely due to a change in the environment. Say, for example, that an unruly child acts out in the presence of its parents but is quiet and well mannered in school. The marked difference in behavior, while laudable when it occurs, does not represent true growth of the child as a person, since the behavior is contingent on environmental influences.

Finally, if a child learns to control its outbursts at home and at school, the observable, lasting improvement in behavior does, in fact, represent a change in the person that is independent of the environment and, hence, represents true human development.

Whereas these two simple measurement constructs of the human development model serve to distinguish true personal growth from temporary behavioral change, they do not, in and of themselves, help to explain why human beings develop. As the next section will clarify, a causative engine must drive human development.

Causes of Human Development

The views of various theorists on human development are best understood if viewed from a consistent framework. The second part of the human development model incorporates such a framework or perspective; namely, that human development results from (a) the operation of certain driving forces (b) through a variety of processes (c) toward an end goal. For example, Freud (1962/2000) essentially viewed human development as the result of (a) instinctual desires (sex and aggression), (b) governed by the id, ego, and superego, (c) toward the goal of functioning with restraint and getting things done by balancing these three systems (i.e., id, ego, and superego) effectively.

Table 1 summarizes the ideas of five important thinkers on the subject of human development. The rest of this section discusses the ideas of each theorist in more detail in an effort to answer the question: What causes human development?

Table 1—Theories of Human Development

Theorist	Driving Forces	Process	Goal
Maslow	Positive, uniquely human motives, such as helping others	Satisfying a hierarchy of needs	Self-actualization
Erikson	Instincts, plus social interactions and experiences	Resolution of life crises associated with specific stages	Ego integrity in the final stage of life
Hudson	Interaction of personal desire to grow with social forces	Personal mastery of cycle of change and life cycle	Ongoing self-renewal
Kegan	Need to evolve in consciousness to make sense of life	Process of learning to cope with the environment	Match mental capabilities to demands of the culture
Bronfen-brenner	Change behavior by changing the systems in the environment	Interaction between the systems and the person	Better systems foster develop-ment

Maslow

Maslow (1954/1987) is most well known for his theory of the hierarchy of needs, which is the focus of this section. The stages in the human development model, which consist of driving forces, change process, and the end goal of development, provide a framework for examining this and other important theories of human motivation and development.

Maslow (1954/1987) postulated that human needs fall into five categories: physiological, safety, love, esteem, and self-actualization. In terms of the differences between higher and lower order needs in this hierarchy, Maslow (1954/1987) stated that:

> The basic needs arrange themselves in a fairly definite hierarchy on the basis of relative potency. Thus the safety need is stronger than the love need because it dominates the organism in various demonstrable ways when both needs are frustrated. In this sense, the physiological needs (which are themselves ordered in a subhierarchy) are stronger than the safety needs, which are stronger than the love needs, which in turn are stronger than the esteem needs, which are stronger than those idiosyncratic needs we have called the need for self-actualization. (p. 56–57).

The second part of Maslow's theory is that a satisfied need is not a motivator of behavior. This so-called deficit principle helps identify what level a person is operating at and provides valuable clues as to what might motivate the behavior of that individual. For example, a person who is not hungry, and feels safe, loved, and respected is free to self-actualize (i.e., to grow and use abilities to their fullest and most creative extent). Whereas, someone who is not loved will find the need to satisfy this longing for affection and a sense of belonging dominates their attention and, to a great extent, determines behavior.

To Maslow (1954/1987, p. 57–58), there were numerous benefits to attaining the highest order state of self-actualization, including:

1. "Living at the higher need level means greater biological efficiency, greater longevity, less disease, better sleep, appetite, and so on."

2. "Higher need gratifications produce more desirable subjective results, that is, more profound happiness, serenity, and richness of the inner life."

3. "Pursuit and gratification of higher needs present represent a general healthward trend, a trend away from psychopathology."

4. "The pursuit and gratification of the higher needs have desirable civic and social consequences. To some extent, the higher the need the less selfish it must be."

5. "The pursuit and gratification of the higher needs leads to greater, stronger, and truer individual-

> ism . . . . People living at the level of self-actualization are, in fact, found simultaneously to love mankind most and to be the most developed idiosyncratically. This supports Fromm's contention that self-love (or better, self-respect) is synergic with rather than antagonistic to love for others."

In summary, Maslow believed that the need, as one matures, to progress from lower level to higher level needs in search of the ultimate goal of self-actualization drives human development.

Erikson

Erikson, a student of Freud, believed that human beings develop by facing and resolving a series of life crises associated with specific stages or times in life. But Erikson believed that development occurred not only during childhood, but also over the course of the entire life span, and not only as a result of internal work, but also as a result of important social interactions and other external experiences.

Erikson (1997) theorized that there are eight distinct stages of development, which he called "the eight ages of man." Associated with each stage is a life crisis that the individual must resolve effectively to avoid maladjustment and difficulties at later stages in life. Unlike Freud, Erikson believed that people are not passively at the mercy of their unconscious instincts but can act rationally (i.e., consciously) to resolve the life crises engendered by these instincts and, thereby, contribute to their own development.

Table 2, excerpted from Chart 1 on pages 33 and 34 of Erikson (1997), summarizes the eight stages, the life crisis associated with each, and the people in the environment most directly involved at each stage.

Table 2—Erikson's Eight Ages of Man Theory

	Stage Name	**Psycho-sexual Mode**	**Psycho-social Crisis**	**Social Context**
I	Infancy	Oral	Trust vs. Mistrust	Maternal Person
II	Childhood	Anal	Autonomy vs. Shame, Doubt	Parental Persons
III	Play Age	Infantile Genital	Initiative vs. Guilt	Basic Family
IV	School Age	Latency	Industry vs. Inferiority	Neighborhood, School
V	Adoles-cence	Puberty	Identity vs. Role Confusion	Peer Groups, Leadership Models
VI	Young Adulthood	Genitality	Intimacy vs. Isolation	Partners in sex, friend-ship, etc.
VII	Adulthood	Procreativ-ity	Generativity vs. Stagnation	Divided labor and Shared household
VIII	Old Age	Generaliza-tion	Integrity vs. Despair	Mankind, My Kind

By meeting the challenge posed by each life crisis, an individual gains a basic human strength ("ego quality"). Psychological strengths, such as hope, purpose, competence, and love "emerge from the struggles of syntonic and dystonic tendencies at...crucial stages of life" (Erikson, 1997, p. 55). As a result of effective maternal care, the child develops in infancy trust in the world and hope. In childhood, the infant develops a sense of autonomy, as evidenced in an ability to dress and eat, resulting in the development of purpose. At the age of play, the child learns to take initiative in ways that do not infringe on the rights of others, thus avoiding punishment and feelings of guilt. This results in the development of purpose. At school age, the child finds itself increasingly in competition with others and, if successful, develops a sense of work/industry resulting in the emergence of competence.

During adolescence, a person struggles with issues of identity and emergences with a greater sense of fidelity. As a young adult, a person forms close friendships and achieves marital intimacy. The result is the emergence of (the ability to) love as a psychological strength. In adulthood, a person raises a family, works productively, and develops the capacity to care. Finally, in old age, a person achieves wisdom by integrating the work of the previous stages. As with all of the stages, failure to resolve the crisis effectively has consequences. In this case, the result of failure to find the meaning in life is despair. The ultimate goal of life is to live in a way that will make life, when viewed in retrospect, seem worthwhile. And, favorably resolving the unique crisis of each age is the way to maximize the likelihood of leading a successful (worthwhile) life.

Thus, for Erikson the cumulative effect of this ongoing process of facing and meeting the psychosocial crisis of each life stage was human development, and the end result was the achievement of the wisdom and ego integrity associated with the last stage of life (old age).

Hudson

In contrast to Erikson, who as a disciple of Freud basically extended Freud's theories in creative and powerful ways, Hudson (1999) was a disciple of Carl Jung.

> Unlike Freud, who viewed human life as shaped through psychosexual stages in the early years of life, Jung portrayed the second half of life as a time of immense growth and development, particularly for personal introspection, reevaluation, and spiritual discovery . . . . I have found that much of the Jungian material speaks to people in midlife, which he viewed as the ripening of the inner, adult self in the second half of life. (Hudson, 1999, p. xii)

Hudson (1999) argued against stage theories of development in favor of a "maturational process" across the life cycle that focuses on the "interaction between developmental events and the social forces that surround them" arguing that "social forces of change are now major sources of personal change and development and can be neither subordinated to normative age periods nor distilled into more predicable events" (p. xiii)

According to Hudson (1999), the process by which development occurs is one of continuous personal cycles (not the linear stages of earlier theorists like Erikson) operating within ongoing social change. Hudson (1999) suggested that "throughout the life cycle, adults keep rearranging the same basic life issues (such as identity, achievement, intimacy, play and creativity, search for meaning, and contribution) around changing perspectives that our personal development, aging, and social conditions evoke from us" (p. xiii). Hence, the cycle of personal change occurs within the larger, ongoing life cycle. And, when properly managed, the process leads to human development in the form of ongoing self-renewal.

It is important to note the five major characteristics of the cycle of personal change that differentiate it from the linear view of traditional stage theories and represent the unique contribution of this theory. Hudson (1999, pp. 43–45) asserted that:

1. "First, it portrays life as a complex, pluralistic, multivariate flow, with ongoing cycles in nature, societies, and people." Thus, development for adults is about "adaptation to change—change within themselves and within their environment."

2. "Second, the cyclical picture assumes that life 'develops' through cycles of change and continuity rather than in progressive, linear, straight lines."

3. "Third, the cyclical picture honors both the ups and downs of life, the blessings and the curses. Conflict and loss are part of everyday life. Both

are incorporated into the way we life and interact with one another."

4. "Fourth, the cyclical view portrays our human systems as modular, flexible, interactive, conflictual, and resilient, permitting continuous adaptations ..... Adults learn to shape and adapt to these systems in different ways at different times and places."

5. "Fifth, continuous learning is essential to the constant retooling of adult competence .... As they age, adults need to unlearn old habits and learn new ways to live effectively."

This cyclical view of the personal change process, based as it is on the Jungian view of the "collective unconscious" as a guide to human development, coupled with the ongoing impact of changing social forces (the other key feature of the Hudson model) has much to offer as a foundation for a macro view of human development.

Kegan

Kegan (1994), an educator by occupation, used the analogy of a curriculum to make sense of the many demands placed on human beings by the modern world. Suggesting that adulthood may not be an end state but "a vast evolutionary expanse encompassing a variety of capacities of mind," Kegan (1994) focused on "the curriculum of modern life in relation to the capacities of the adult mind" (p. 5). In so doing, Kegan (1994) attempted an integration of the literatures of the disparate disciplines that focus on human development, from management to parenting, for the purpose of creating a more coherent view of contemporary adulthood.

Kegan (1994) used as an analytical tool to examine contemporary culture, a theory of the development of human consciousness "that considers not only people's changing agendas but their changing capacities" (p. 7). Kegan based this theory of human development on the work of Piaget, who viewed the cognitive development of a child over time as divisible into a series of stages the products of which included the development of moral reasoning and a sense of self. However, Kegan (1994) extended the work of Piaget in several important ways:

> I looked at psychological growth as the unselfconscious development of successively more complex principles for organizing experience. Building on the work of Piaget and those who came after him, I took the idea of such principles of mental organization and extended its "breadth" (beyond thinking to affective, interpersonal, and intrapersonal realms) and its "length" (beyond childhood and adolescence to adulthood). (p. 29)

According to the subject-object theory of Kegan (1994), there are five levels of ability that human beings use to organize their experience, called organizing principles. Each level or category represents a level of consciousness that is achieved in a given stage (age range). And each category or level is characterized in three domains: (a) cognitive, (b) intrapersonal-affective, and (c) sociocognitive. Finally, the higher the level, the higher the level of development exhibited by the individual.

1. "The first and least complex of these (organizing) principles is the one most commonly used by young children, the principle of *independent elements*. Their attachment to the momentary, the immediate, and the atomistic makes their thinking fantastic and illogical, their feelings impulsive and fluid, and their social-relating egocentric" (p. 29).

2. "The second of these principles is the *durable category*, the principle children usually evolve in latency" (p. 29) At this level, thinking becomes "more concrete and logical, their feelings to be made up of time-enduring needs and dispositions rather than momentary impulses, and their social-relating to grant to themselves and others a separate mind and a distinct point of view" (p. 29).

3. The third category is *cross-categorical knowing* or meaning-making. At this level, the adolescent develops the capacity to think abstractly, have feelings that are a matter of inner states (such as self-confidence and guilt), and their social skills now include the ability to show loyalty to an idea or community larger than the self.

4. The fourth level of development is *systems/complex*. At this stage, the adult develops the ability to thinking systemically (i.e., about

systems and their component sub-systems), to have feelings that reflect self-regulation, autonomy, and individuation, and social-relating skills that reflect consciousness of the social demands of playing multiple roles in complex organizations.

5. The fifth order of consciousness is the *trans-system, trans-complex.* Most closely associated with postmodernism, this order is difficult to understand and even more difficult to attain. Kegan (1994) says that "the fifth order moves form or system from subject to object, and brings into being a new 'trans-system' or 'cross-form' way of organizing reality" thus creating a "context for a sharing and an interacting in which (people) are helped to experience their 'multipleness,' in which the *many* forms or systems that each self is are helped to emerge" (pp. 312–313).

Fortunately for mere mortals, Kegan concludes that fifth order consciousness is not yet a requirement for coping with life in the new millennium. For now, human beings can content themselves with augmenting their analytical thinking with (the now required) systems thinking capabilities of fourth–order consciousness.

In summary, Kegan (1994) maintained that the demands of modern life force human beings to develop or evolve to higher and higher orders of consciousness by means of an ongoing process of interactions between the individual and the surrounding social and cultural systems.

Bronfenbrenner

Like Kegan, Bronfenbrenner (1979) believed that the environment plays a pivotal role in human development: "Human abilities and their realization depend in significant degree on the larger social and institutional context of individual activity" (p. xv). In contrast to Kegan, whose theories are both abstruse and hard to apply, Bronfenbrenner wrote in a crisp and lucid style that informs and captures the imagination. As will become clear, the theories of Bronfenbrenner (1979) have a great deal to offer about what causes human development.

Bronfenbrenner built his theory of human development on the ideas of Kurt Lewin about the life space (i.e., psychological field):

> Lewin maintained that applications of field theory were possible in all branches of psychology. He viewed the life space as the psychologist's universe. In it, person and environment are interrelated and individual behavior is always derived from the relation of the concrete individual to the concrete situation. Behavior, therefore, is a function of the life space: B = f(LS), which in turn is a product of the interaction between the person, P, and his (or her) environment, E. (Marrow, 1969, p. 38)

However, Bronfenbrenner greatly expanded the role of the environment in human development by applying notions of systems theory to its explication. Bronfenbrenner (1979) offered a new "conception of the developing person, of the environment, and especially of the evolving interaction between the two." To Bronfenbrenner, development was "a lasting change in the way in which a person perceives and deals with his environment" (p. 3).

Bronfenbrenner defined the environment from an ecological perspective; that is, in terms of the relationship between the organism (individual) and its environment. "The ecological environment is conceived as a set of nested structures, each inside the next, like a set of Russian dolls" (Bronfenbrenner, 1979, p. 3).

Briefly, the inner most level (the microsystem) contains the individual and the people in the immediate surroundings (like the home and the parents); the next level (the mesosystem) consists of those systems (and the people in them) with whom the individual has frequent and important interactions (like home and parents, and school and teachers, or work and colleagues); a third level (the exosystem) includes people and events who influence the individual but are not, in turn, influenced by the individual (such as the workplace of the parents in the case of a child); and the final level (the macrosystem) is the culture or broader society that surrounds the individual but is does not directly influence the individual on a regular basis (such as the legal system or the American way of life).

Acknowledging that his concept of the environment was "somewhat unorthodox," Bronfenbrenner (1979) nonetheless asserted that it was a necessary construct to overcome the tendency of researchers to overemphasize the personal aspects of development at the expense of the environmental impacts and the interaction between the two:

> What we find in practice, however, is a marked asymmetry, a hypertrophy of theory and research focusing on the properties of the person and only the most rudimentary conception and characterization of the environment in which the person is found. (p. 16)

Regardless of his reasons for developing such an elaborate model for the environment, in so doing Bronfenbrenner added a much needed systems perspective to what is clearly a systemic situation, the ongoing development of a human being. As Bronfenbrenner (1979) so eloquently stated:

> To assert that human development is a product of the interaction between the growing human organism and its environment is to state what is almost commonplace in behavioral science. It is a proposition that all students of behavior would find familiar, with which none would take issue, and that few would regard as in any way remarkable, let alone revolutionary, in its scientific implications. (p 16)

So Bronfenbrenner saw the environment, the immediate setting in which a person lives and its supersystems, as a critical element in human development. To make this more specific, consider the definition of microsystem offered by Bronfenbrenner (1979): "A microsystem is a pattern of activities, roles, and interpersonal relations experienced by the developing person in a given (physical) setting" (p. 22).

One very important aspect of this definition is captured by the word "experienced." Bronfenbrenner (1979) argued strongly that, in effect, perception is reality:

> Very few of the external influences significantly affecting human behavior and development can be described solely in terms of objective physical conditions and events; the aspects of the environment that are most powerful in shaping the course of psychological growth are overwhelmingly those that have meaning to the person in a given situation. (p. 22)

One other important characteristic of the environment in the Bronfenbrenner (1979) theory is the notion of "ecological transition," which is "a general phenomenon of movement through ecological space" that is "both a product and a producer of developmental change." More formally, "an ecological transition occurs whenever a person's position in the ecological environment is altered as the result of a change in role, setting, or both" (p. 22). These transitions occur frequently and mark the occasions of development for an individual. For example, attending (or graduating) from school, accepting (or quitting) a job, and marrying (or divorcing) are ecological transitions that have major development opportunities associated with them.

Bronfenbrenner (1979) encapsulated all of these concepts into a single definition of human development that incorporates its driving forces, ongoing process, and desired outcome:

> Human development is the process through which the growing person acquires a more extended, differentiated, and valid conception of the ecological environment, and becomes motivated and able to engage in activities that reveal the properties of, sustain, or restructure that environment at levels of similar or greater complexity in form and content. (p. 27)

In summary, according to Bronfenbrenner (1979), to catalyze human development, change the systems in the environment of the person for the better. The corresponding interaction between the environment and the person will take the form of either a change in role or setting and will result in an ecological transition to a higher order environment. If the personal motivation to change is present, the result will be individual growth/development.

For example, if you want your child to learn to read better and faster, read to him or her and make it fun. This favorable change in their mesosystem (which constitutes a change in the role of the child from non-listener to active listener and participant in the process), will encourage an ecological transition (in all likelihood the child will become motivated to learn to read on its own). The result will be human development.

Consider a slightly more elaborate example concerning the effect of a change in the federal laws designed to eliminate all vestiges of the glass ceiling in organizations. This change in the macrosystem, assuming effective implementation, would result in workplace changes (the exosystem) that could improve the circumstances and attitude of a parent, which in turn could impact the microsystem of a child positively. Say, for example, the affected parent earned a higher salary as a result of the new laws and could afford to spend more time at home with the child. The end result could easily be more rapid growth of the child attributable directly to a favorable change in the ecological environment.

This overview of major human development theorists, such as Maslow, Erikson, and Bronfenbrenner, begs the question of whether a creative synthesis of their ideas into a single macro theory is possible.

Integrated View of Human Development

Recall that the human development model described earlier requires that a change in behavior be measurable, positive, lasting, and primarily attributable to a change in the person, not to constraints placed on an individual by the environment.

Taking these as building blocks for a macro theory of human development, the operative question is: What do the great theorists have to offer by way of enhancements to this rudimentary model?

Freud (1962/2000) proposed that development at times results from internal, unconscious, instinctual forces. This has much intuitive appeal and, therefore, belongs in the macro model. Vaillant (1993), a disciple of Freud, pointed out that people and other external realities in the environment of an individual are important forces that stimulate or motivate change. So they too belong in the macro model. Furthermore, as Bronfenbrenner suggested, the environment is not some amorphous cloud surrounding the individual, but an interconnected series of systems that interact with the individual to foster development. This notion of the ecological environment is extremely powerful and, therefore, also belongs in the macro model.

Having ensured the presence in the macro model of a strong component representing the environment and environmental influences on human development, the next step is to examine the role of personal or internal factors in the process of change. First, imagine that Freud and Maslow are like opponents in a debate arguing, respectively, that human beings are at the mercy of their baser instincts or that they are free to capitalize on the loving nature of all human beings to develop themselves to the highest degree possible.

Which of these points of view about human nature is correct? Without being facetious, the answer is both. The macro model must reflect the yin and yang of every human being. Therefore, the appropriate response is to take a page out of Vaillant (1993) and combine it with Bronfenbrenner (1979) to acknowledge that while human beings are at times motivated by inner, often basic instincts, such as sex and aggression, which create serious conflicts that demand resolution, they are also abetted at these times by the forces of conscience, people, other aspects of the *ecological* environment, and ego that are simultaneously at work to mitigate and channel the outcome.

Conversely, there are times when development is motivated by the desire to learn or grow (in a positive way) either to adapt to an environmental challenge (ecological transition) or for self-enrichment or self-renewal. At these times, Maslow, Hudson (and Jung), and Kegan suggest that the cycle of change that occurs allows the individual to achieve an even higher level of consciousness. So, to be complete, the macro model must allow for this undeniable yin and yang of human motivation.

Another important element of the macro model is whether or not it is a stage model. Hudson, Kegan, and Bronfenbrenner provided clues to the efficacy of a stage model when designed to avoid some of the obvious pitfalls of earlier conceptions, like those of Freud and Erikson. The latter theorists focused too much on the stages as the driving forces of change and too little on the stages as convenient categories to capture significant commonalities across a broad spectrum of human beings.

By taking into account explicitly the cyclical (as opposed to linear) nature of growth, the natural tendency to seek higher levels of consciousness to be able to cope with the constantly increasing demands of life over the life span, and the significant impact of the environment on human development, Hudson, Kegan, and Bronfenbrenner have elevated this essential element of any macro model (i.e., stages) to its appropriate stage of evolution.

The final element of the macro model is the goal or desired outcome of human development. To this end, the notions of ongoing self-renewal (Hudson), self-actualization (Maslow), and achieving a state of ego integrity and wisdom (Erikson) belong in the model.

In summary, the macro model proposed here (a) views the driving forces of human development as the tension or conflict that arises from internal and internal sources (primarily desire, conscience, people, and the rest of the ecological environment) as a result of a gap between the current reality of the individual and the desired end state or goal; (b) views the process of development as progressing in stages and cycles throughout the life span of the individual based on the interaction, at key times, of the person and the multiphase environment (microsystem, mesosystem, exosystem, and macrosystem), either in reaction to events or in response to ecological transitions; and (c) views the ultimate goal of human development as the highest possible state of human consciousness attainable, including but not limited to the goals of ongoing self-renewal, self-actualization, and the attainment of wisdom.

It is this highest order human need that the modern leadership model attempts to address directly by crystallizing a "collective purpose" and enabling a shared effort to attain it.

Appendix B

Leadership Theories

How does the modern, transformative leadership and change model presented in this book relate to other conceptions of leadership and change?

To answer this question, in this appendix we examine some important classic and contemporary leadership theories.

Historical Perspectives on Leadership

Based on primarily on Daft (1999) and Schermerhorn (2001), the following briefly summarizes the major leadership theories that have captured the attention of leaders and leadership researchers over the years. These theories focus, respectively, on traits, behavior, situational responses, and charisma of the leader. The purpose of this overview is to provide a context for the emergence of the modern leadership model described in chapters 1 to 6.

Trait Theories

According to Daft (1999), the Greeks spoke of heroes (such as Hercules) in their myths. More recently, great men like Julius Caesar, Napoleon, George Washington, Abraham Lincoln, Gandhi, and Martin Luther King, Jr. were apparently born to lead due to their intelligence, self-confidence, drive, and other personal characteristics. If they set a direction, people would follow them. In terms of leadership development, "the dominance of these great figures spurred research into 'traits' that comprised a leader. People thought that if traits could be identified, leaders could be predicted or perhaps trained" (Daft, 1999, p. 48).

Despite the widespread belief that possessing the traits of the great leaders is an indicator of leadership ability, the research literature does not support this conclusion:

> Most of the evidence of such characteristics must be labeled moot. Scores of studies have been conducted.

> Researchers have compared bishops and clergy, insurance executives and policyholders, military officers and recent recruits. They have examined people whose careers boomed and those whose careers "went bust." They have studied old and young, men and women—all in wide variety of organizational settings. Despite all this work, the most optimistic claim possible is that consistent evidence of individual characteristics that cause leadership has not yet emerged. (Hornstein, Heilman, Mone, & Tartell, 1987, pp. 56–57)

Nevertheless, the belief that a "savior" like John F. Kennedy or Jack Welch will appear to lead society or an organization out of the darkness, persists today among boards of directors, stockholders, employees, and the general public, particularly in this era of disconcerting, discontinuous change

Behavioral Theories

If successful leaders are not born, what do they do that makes them successful? The behavioral theorists argue that leadership style is the key to leadership effectiveness. As defined by Schermerhorn (2001), "leadership style is the recurring pattern of behaviors exhibited by a leader" (p. 267). According to Daft (1999), groundbreaking experiments by Kurt Lewin on autocratic versus democratic leadership styles led to refinements by Tannenbaum and Schmidt, whose research showed "that leadership behavior could exist on a continuum reflecting different amounts of employee participation. Thus, one leader might be autocratic (boss-centered), another democratic (subordinate-centered), and a third a mix of the two styles" (Daft, 1999, pp. 69-71).

According to Daft (1999), Blake and Mouton developed the "Leadership Grid" to depict the two dimensions of a theory which assumes that leadership style is a function of (a) "concern for production" (task) and (b) "concern for people." The so-called 9,9 manager or high task-high people leader hopes to encourage team management by behaving in this way. The underlying belief of the 9,9 leader is that "work accomplishment is from committed people; interdependence through a 'common stake' in organization purpose leads to relationships of trust and respect" (Daft, 1999, p. 76).

While each of these behavioral theories of leadership has its adherents, many people question the wisdom of employing one leadership style all of the time. For example, if a democratic leadership style works well in a stable situation with knowledge workers, will it work as well in a crisis or with inflexible union workers? The next generation of theories revolves around the idea that the situation determines the most effective leadership style to use.

According to Daft (1999), the migration from behavioral to situational theories of leadership and leadership development represents a paradigm shift from "universalistic" approaches (based on traits and behaviors) to "contingency" approaches (based on the interaction of the leader, the followers, and the situation) (p. 93).

Contingency Theories

Daft (1999) describes several of the most important of the situational or contingency leadership theories by Fiedler, Vroom, and Hersey and Blanchard. The Fiedler and Vroom models, which are quite complicated, view leadership style (the dependent variable) as a function of the followers and the situation (the independent variables). A simpler and better-known model by Hersey and Blanchard prescribes the optimum leadership style (either telling, selling, participating, or delegating) as a function of the readiness of the followers only. Basically, Hersey-Blanchard postulate that each leadership style (i.e., combination of task and leadership behavior) is best suited to a state of follower readiness (to take responsibility for their work).

According to the theory, low readiness (R1) followers are "unable and unwilling or insecure." Therefore, a directive, "telling" style characterized by a high degree of task focus and a low degree of affective or relationship behavior is called for. A less task focused (directive) and more supportive (higher relationship behavior) called "selling" is called for if the followers are "unable but willing or confident" (R2).

For followers with a higher readiness (R3), a "participating" style (which is high in relationship behavior and lower in task behavior "that focuses on supporting the growth and improvement of others") is most appropriate. Finally, a "delegating" style that is low in relationship and low in task behavior works best for followers who are at the highest level of readiness (R4) and are, therefore, "able and willing or confident" (Daft, 1999, p.100).

Interestingly, Hornstein et al. (1987) conducted an experiment involving 150 men and women from a large company to test the efficacy of the Hersey-Blanchard model. The findings are revealing: "Generally, people viewed high relationship leader behavior as more organizationally beneficial than low relationship behavior...Therefore, we did not find evidence to support the idea that following the situational leadership model enhances the perception of leader effectiveness" (Hornstein et al., 1987, p. 60).

Research findings suggest that complicated, overly prescriptive (normative) theories/models of situational leadership stimulate negative responses from employees who prefer positive, supportive, participative leadership styles. According to Johnson and Johnson (1997), an army of researchers has shown that such cooperative styles are far more effective in producing high performance as well as high member satisfaction than competitive/autocratic leadership styles. So while situational leadership theories may have appeal to leaders and researchers, suggesting the perceptiveness and versatility of the leader, they may not work as well in practice. If so, what other theories, contingency based or not, exist to guide the would-be leader?

Charismatic Theories

Visionary leadership, transformational leadership, ethical leadership, and servant leadership are among the new wave of inspirational and empowering leadership theories that have emerged recently in response to the need to engage all of the members of a system (i.e., group, organization, community, or society) in a coordinated response to the rapid, discontinuous changes occurring in all facets of the environment (political, social, economic, cultural, technological, and legal) today.

The great man trait leadership theorists were the first to lay claim to the idea that a leader must inspire the followers. They believed that the personal characteristics of the leader would be sufficient to accomplish this important objective. Another way to achieve this end, one that requires the leader to be more thoughtful but not as heroic in stature or charismatic in speech, is by creating a concrete, compelling vision of the future. When properly painted, such a big picture engages, empowers, and energizes the members of the system (e.g., employees, volunteers, or citizens) to achieve it. The name of the theory that supports leaders in developing such visions and enrolling others in them is visionary leadership (Bradford & Cohen, 1984; Senge, 1990).

Transformational leadership, a theory developed by Bernard Bass in the eighties, distinguishes between so called transactional leaders (who focus on doing things right) and transformational leaders (who focus on doing the right things). The former strive to optimize present organizational efficiency, while the latter strive to maximize future organizational effectiveness.

According to Daft (1999), transformational leaders enable and manage change by (a) developing followers into leaders, (b) elevating followers concerns from basic needs (like safety and security) to higher level needs (like self-actualization), (c) inspiring followers to work for the good of the group, and (d) creating a vision of the future that "makes the pain of change worth the effort" (p. 428). To a certain extent, transformational leadership subsumes visionary leadership, at least in the sense that vision plays an important role in initiating the transformation.

Ethical leadership is less a theory than a call to action. According to Daft (1999), it is about morality, integrity, and doing the right thing. In the aftermath of recent Enron and WorldCom scandals, the appeal of ethical leadership is stronger than ever. According to Schermerhorn (2001), "leaders have an undeniable responsibility to set high ethical standards to guide the behavior of followers. For managers, the ethical aspects of leadership are important and everyday concerns" (p. 277). Clearly, a strong ethical focus is an essential element of any theory of leadership, whether it is top-down or transformational or anything in between.

Servant leadership is one of the latest theories to capture the attention of contemporary leaders and their followers. This revolutionary concept views the leader as the servant to the organization, which, in turn, serves the customers, clients, or (more generally) the stakeholders. This is the exact opposite of the traditional, top-down organizational view that the employees at the bottom of the organizational pyramid exist to support their bosses, who, in turn, support the leader, who sits at the top of the pyramid. In the traditional organization, the lower level employees are the servants.

According to Daft (1999), the tenets of servant leadership are (a) put service before self-interest, (b) listen first to affirm others, (c) inspire trust by being trustworthy, and (d) nourish others and help them to become whole (p. 375). While these behaviors are extraordinary, laudable, and doable, they are not sufficient by themselves to constitute a theory of leadership. Like ethical leadership, they are a call to action.

If not traits, behavior, situations, or charisma per se, then what defines the true leader, particularly one who would lead in the 21st century? The chapters of this book attempt to answer this important question.

Appendix C

OD & Change Management

What is Organization Development (OD)?

According to Burke (1987), "organization development is a planned process of change in an organization's culture through the utilization of behavioral science technologies, research, and theory" (p. 11).

Organization development has two basic goals. First, to improve outcomes by focusing on tasks. Second, to enhance the way people work together by focusing on process. Organization development consultants pursue both—task and process—simultaneously in every OD intervention/change effort.

To effect change, organization development consultants work with organizational leaders to design and plan interventions, which are action steps designed to help an organization move in a specific, desired direction. According to Burke (1987, pp. 54–62), the process of planned change, which is based on the methodology of action research, has eight steps. These steps, in turn, incorporate the Lewin three-stage model of unfreezing, movement, and refreezing. At the core of the process is the belief that participative processes permit individuals to accept, internalize, and initiate change.

According to Burke (1987, p. 61), the eights steps of the action research model are: (a) perception of the problem, (b) consultant entry, (c) data collection, and (d) feedback to the client to unfreeze the situation; (e) joint action planning and (f) action to move or change; and (g) assessment and (h) feedback to the client to refreeze the situation or initiate another change cycle. Note that "in practice, the words action research are reversed . . . for initially research is first conducted and then action is taken as a direct result of what the research data are interpreted to indicate" (Burke, 1987, p. 54).

It is important to give credit to Kurt Lewin, the man who developed the action research process and conducted many projects using it. "Although Lewin was an academician . . . he was just as eminent a man of action...Moreover, he pulled it together when he stated that there is 'no action without research, and no research without action" (Burke, 1987, p. 54).

As the above indicates, action research in the form of an OD planned change effort rests on the belief that change is a collaborative process. Underlying this belief is the assumption that people will change if the process treats them honestly and with respect. In practice, this amounts to designing and implementing a change management process that treats everyone involved, from the CEO to the janitor, as a human being with important feelings, rights, and ideas that are just as important as the organizational goals, such as improved productivity, profit, or market share, that the change effort is intended to produce.

Organization development consultants imbue their work with these dual objectives (i.e., achieving organizational objectives by involving people in the change process) for two reasons: (a) because it is the right thing to do and (b) because it works. Involved employees are more motivated and less resistant to change than employees who are told that they will have to change or else. Furthermore, the changes committed employees make last longer than those imposed from above.

As the people in the OD community realize, the secret to better individual, team, and overall organizational performance is true collaboration, not coercion or competition.

References

Abrashoff, D. M. (2001). Retention through redemption. *Harvard Business Review, 79*(2), 136–141.

Abshire, D. M. (2001). A call for transformational leadership. *Vital Speeches of the Day, 67*(14), 432–435.

Ackoff, R. L. (1999). Transformational leadership. *Strategy and Leadership, 27*(1), 20–25.

Argyris, C., & Schon, D. A. (1978). *Organizational learning.* Reading, Mass.: Addison-Wesley.

Avolio, B. J., Waldman, D. A., & Yammarino, F. J. (1991). Leading in the 1990's: The four I's of transformational leadership. *Journal of European Industrial Training, 15*(4), 9–16.

Bass, B. M. (1990). From transactional to transformational leadership: Learning to share the vision. *Organizational Dynamics, 18*(3), 19–31.

Bennis, W. (1999). New leadership. *Executive Excellence, 16*(11), 7–8.

Bertalanffy, L. (1968). *General systems theory: Foundations, development, applications* (Revised ed.). New York: G. Braziller.

Blubaugh, D. (2002). The blind men and the elephant. Peace Corps Coverdell World Wise Schools. Retrieved June 8, 2005, from http://www.peacecorps.gov/wws/guides/looking/story22.html.

Boyer, E. L. (1990). *Scholarship reconsidered: Priorities of the professoriate.* San Francisco, CA: Jossey-Bass Publishers.

Bradford, D. L., & Cohen, A. R. (1984). *Managing for excellence: The guide to developing high performance in contemporary organizations.* New York: John Wiley & Sons.

Bridges, W. (1980). *Transitions: Making sense of life's changes*. Reading, Massachusetts: Addison-Wesley.

Bridges, W. (1991). *Managing transitions: Making the most of change.* Reading, Massachusetts: Addison-Wesley.

Bronfenbrenner, U. (1979). *The ecology of human development: Experiments by nature and design.* Cambridge, MA: Harvard University Press.

Burke, W. W. (1982). *Organization development: Principles and practices.* Boston: Little, Brown and Company.

Burke, W. W. (1987). *Organization development: A normative view.* Reading, Massachusetts: Addison-Wesley.

Burns, J. M. (1978). *Leadership.* New York: Harper & Row.

Burns, J. M. (2003). *Transforming leadership: A new pursuit of happiness.* New York: Atlantic Monthly Press.

Carl, D. E., & Javidian, M. (2001). Universality of charismatic leadership: A multi-nation study. *Academy of Management Proceedings,* B1–B6.

Cavaleri, S., Seivert, S., & Lee, L. W. (2005). *Knowledge leadership.* Amsterdam: Elsevier.

Cleveland, H. (2000). Coming soon: The nobody-in-charge society. *Futurist, 34*(5), 52–56.

Daft, R. L. (1999). *Leadership: Theory and practice.* Fort Worth: Harcourt, Inc.

Day, G. S. (1999). Creating a market-driven organization. *Sloan Management Review, 41*(1), 11–22.

Elrod II, P. D., & Tippett, D. D. (2002). The 'death valley' of change. *Journal of Organizational Change Management, 15*(3), 273–291.

Erikson, E. H. (1997). *The life cycle completed.* New York: W. W. Norton.

Freud, S. (1962/2000). *Three essays on the theory of sexuality.* New York: Basic Books.

Gronn, P. (1997). Leading for learning: Organizational transformation and the formation of leaders. *Journal of Management Development, 16*(4), 274–283.

Handy, C. (1980). Through the organizational looking glass. *Harvard Business Review, 58*(1), 115–121.

Heifetz, R. A., & Linsky, M. (2002). Surviving leadership. *Harvard Management Update, 7*(3), 3–4.

Hornstein, H. A., Heilman, M. E., Mone, E., & Tartell, R. (1987). Responding to contingent leadership behavior. *Organizational Dynamics, 15*(4), 56–65.

Hudson, F. (1999). *The adult years: Mastering the art of self-renewal.* San Francisco: Jossey-Bass.

Jaffe, D. T., & Scott, C. D. (2000). Change leaders and navigators. *Executive Excellence, 17*(12), 13–14.

Johnson, D. W., & Johnson, R. T. (1989). *Cooperation and competition: Theory and research.* Edina, MN: Interaction Book Company.

Kalagher, J. (2002). How to turn change into opportunity for leadership. *Patient Care Management, 17*(11), 1–3.

Kegan, R. (1994). *In over our heads: The mental demands of modern life.* Cambridge, MA: Harvard University Press.

Kotter, J. P. (1996). *Leading change.* Boston: Harvard Business School Press.

Kotter, J. P., & Cohen, D. S. (2002). Putting the gloves on. *Across the Board, 39*(6), 8–9.

Kuhn, T. S. (1962/2004). *The structure of scientific revolutions.* Chicago: The University of Chicago Press.

Laszlo, E. (1996). *The systems view of the world: A holistic vision for our time.* Cresskill, NJ: Hampton Press.

Louis, M. R. (1994). In the manner of friends: Learnings from Quaker practice for organizational renewal. *Journal of Organizational Change Management, 7*(1), 42–60.

Marrow, A. J. (1969). *The practical theorist: The life and work of Kurt Lewin.* New York: Basic Books.

Maslow, A. (1954/1987). *Motivation and personality.* New York: Harper and Row.

Neal, C., & Conhaim, W. (2000). Moving beyond change: An opportunity to transform our organizations. *Journal for Quality & Production, 23*(4), 64.

Schein, E. H. (1999). Kurt Lewin's change theory in the field and in the classroom: Notes toward a model of managed learning. *Reflections: The SOL Journal, 1*(1), 59–74.

Senge, P. M. (1990). *The fifth discipline: The art and practice of the learning organization.* New York: Doubleday.

Shakespeare, W. (1960). *Romeo and Juliet.* New York: Penguin.

Schermerhorn, J. R. (2001). *Management* (6th ed.). New York: John Wiley & Sons, Inc.

Somerset, F. (2001). The softer side of leadership. *CMA Management, 75*(7), 12–13.

Vaillant, G. E. (1993). *The wisdom of the ego.* Cambridge, MA: Harvard University Press.

Weidman, D. (2002). Redefining leadership for the 21st century. *Journal of Business Strategy, 23*(5), 16–18.

Weisbord, M. R., & Janoff, S. (1995). *Future search: An action guide to finding common ground in organizations and communities.* San Francisco: Berrett-Koehler Publishers.

Wiig, K. M. (2004). *People-focused knowledge management*. Amsterdam: Elsevier.

About the Author

Robert E. Levasseur, Ph.D., a full-time faculty member at one of America's premier online Ph.D. granting universities, teaches doctoral courses and mentors Ph.D. students in Leadership and Organizational Change, Information Systems Management, Operations Research, Engineering Management, Accounting, and Knowledge Management.

Dr. Levasseur earned undergraduate degrees in physics and electrical engineering from Bowdoin College and MIT, and master's degrees in electrical engineering and management from Northeastern University and the MIT Sloan School of Management. His Ph.D. is from Walden University.

Dr. Levasseur has taught for Boston University, Anne Arundel Community College, and the University of Maryland University College part-time; and for the University of the Virgin Islands and Walden University full-time.

Dr. Levasseur's professional career spans over three decades and includes leadership, management, and organizational change positions in Fortune 50 corporations. He is a registered Organization Development consultant and a member of INFORMS, the Institute for Operations Research and the Management Sciences.

Dr. Levasseur is the author of numerous articles and books. These include *Breakthrough Business Meetings,*

Leadership and Change in the 21st Century, *Practical Statistics*, and *Student to Scholar*.

A native of Sanford, Maine, Dr. Levasseur and his wife live on the shores of the Chesapeake Bay in Annapolis, Maryland. To learn more about "Dr. L" and his work, visit his web site at www.mindfirepress.com.

Books by Robert E. Levasseur

Breakthrough Business Meetings

Leadership and Change in the 21st Century

Practical Statistics

Student to Scholar

CPSIA information can be obtained at www.ICGtesting.com
Printed in the USA
BVOW02s1137020715

407235BV00001B/9/P